KENT
COUNTRY CHURCHES

First published privately by the author in 1984. This reprint published by Meresborough Books, 7 Station Road, Rainham, Gillingham, Kent. ME8 7RS.

A second volume of drawings, 'Kent Country Churches Continued', is being published by Meresborough Books simultaneously with this reprint at £5.95 (£6.55 by post).

Meresborough Books is a specialist publisher of books on Kent and a monthly magazine 'Bygone Kent' founded in 1979. Among over seventy books currently available is 'Exploring Kent Churches' by John E. Vigar at £3.95 (£4.35 by post). A full list will be sent on request.

ISBN 0948193131

Printed by Whitstable Litho Ltd, Whitstable, Kent.

KENT
COUNTRY CHURCHES

A personal exploration

JAMES ANTONY SYMS

Meresborough Books

CONTENTS

CHURCHES ILLUSTRATED

Iwade	184	Ridley	194
Kemsing	72	Ruckinge	136
Kenardington	138	Seal	16
Knockholt	82	Selling	168
Lamberhurst	54	Sheldwich	178
Leaveland	120	Shoreham	14
Lower Halstow	42	Smeeth	152
Luddenham	162	Snargate	92
Luddesdown	126	Stalisfield	100
Lynsted	76	Stansted	196
Mereworth	202	Sundridge	66
Mersham	154	Teston	200
Meopham	172	Teynham	104
Molash	62	Throwley	102
Norton	180	Tonge	24
Nurstead	108	Trottiscliffe	188
Oare	164	Ulcombe	10
Offham	70	Waltham	156
Old Romney	94	Wateringbury	46
Otford	50	West Kingsdown	114
Otham	110	West Malling	64
Paddlesworth	52	West Peckham	208
Pembury, Old Church	142	Westwell	88
Petham	158	Wickhambreux	36
Pluckley	78	Wrotham	186
Queenborough	184	Wye	128
		Yalding	204

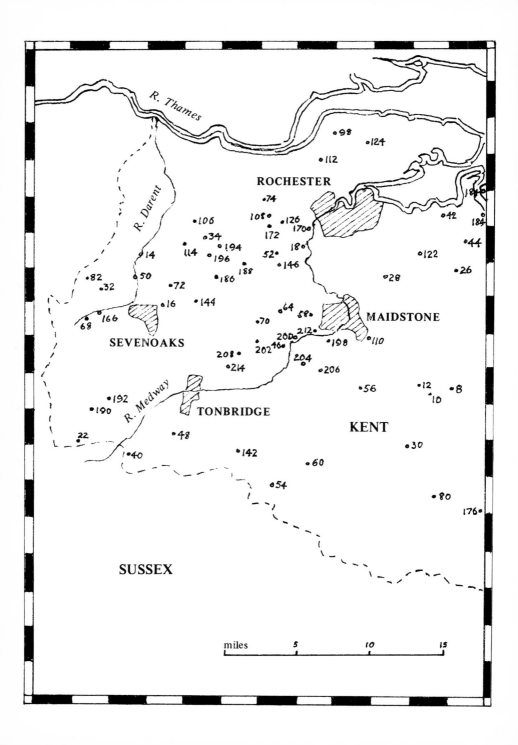

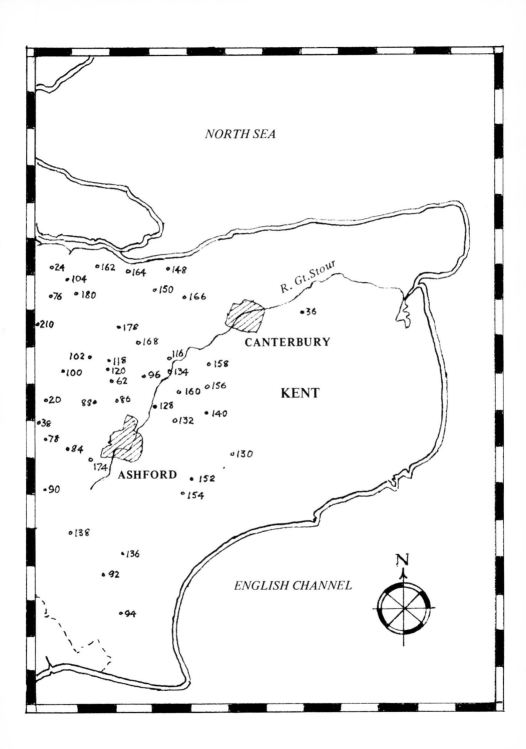

NORTH SEA

R. Gt. Stour

CANTERBURY

KENT

ASHFORD

ENGLISH CHANNEL

N

°24   °162   °164   °148
  °104
°76   °180   °150   °166   °36
°210   °178
            °168
    102 °   °118   °116
  °100   °120   °96 °134   °158
        °62
°20   88°   °86   °160 °156
            °128   °140
°38   °132
°78
  °84   °130
°174
    °152
      °154
  °138
    °136
  °92
    °94

KENT COUNTRY CHURCHES

A personal exploration

When I retired from nine to five employment towards the end of 1978, like anyone else I found myself at last able, within limits, to do what I liked when I liked. A very liberating and stimulating situation to be in at the age of 60 and of relatively sound (some might claim unsound) mind and limb.

Retirement itself initially can prompt something of a stocktaking of one's life. The first realisation it brings is the sobering reflection that one's life has entered its terminal phase; it no longer stretches ahead without conscious end as it did when one was younger. One tends to look back rather than forward and one has to accept that one's years of achievement are behind one. That being so, if one is incautious, one wonders what lasting accomplishments have actually been achieved in one's productive lifetime. Apart from rearing, bringing up and looking after a family, regrettably for most of us and certainly in my case, non-family accomplishments are virtually nil. One has the uncomfortable feeling that in two generations, apart from a name, one will be as completely forgotten and consigned to oblivion as, for instance, is the case with, say, my grandparents vis a vis my children. Observing that we have, I suspect, only one brief moment of animated life in all eternity, it is sad that most of us leave no trace behind apart from our all-important descendants. With someone like Hitler or Genghis Khan, of course, non-performance would have been preferable. But most of us are relatively harmless in our lives and we all aspire to some remembrance, particularly those of us who have made no great stir in this life.

At the risk of striking a depressing note in the introduction to my drawings, perhaps I might expand on this existentialist theme for a moment to explain the motive for this little book. As far as I understand it, existentialism takes the fact of living to be all important and death to be its inevitable and utterly final conclusion. These are the thoughts that tend to occur to people of my age group, always have, and their chilling finality, which can seem to make life pointless, have generally been mitigated in two ways; through religious belief in the hereafter and, more recently and more scientifically, through awareness of the continued existence of the genes that make up our bodies in the bodies of future generations. The objections that cast doubt on these two comforting theories are persuasive, I think. The existence of life after death has never been demonstrated beyond question and certainly not regularly enough to convince the sceptic like myself. Therefore, can one rely on this theory? The presence of all the churches I have drawn, not to mention the countless others, suggests that people have believed in religious immortality in overwhelming numbers. On the other hand, the persistence of genes through generation after generation, barring accidents, confers an immortality of sorts but it is the immortality of the gene not that of the body that housed it temporarily.

The question then is — who am I, or you — a short-term home for some gene or a personality with an identity of its own, a life of its own and an inescapable death to put a full stop to that identity? I wish I could think otherwise than the latter alternative.

Existence of an inanimate character in an individual's hereafter can nevertheless be obtained in two ways; by historical record or by the creation of persistent things bearing his or her signature. Historical record requires achievement in life — in my case, as I say, virtually nil. Creative attainment, at whatever level of competence, may persist and provide that evidence of personal identity which genes in the bodies of future generations never can.

That at least was the way my mind reflected when I looked back at my working life and considered the prospect of the remainder which for the first time had become my own property, free to dispose of as I liked — so I decided that I must try to create some permanent evidence, however imperfect, of my brief existence. In a conventional way, musical composers, authors and artists seem most successful at this; unfortunately musical composition is far out of my reach but art and writing albeit at a pedestrian level offered promise of an accessible route towards my goal of humble immortality. Hence this book.

I have always enjoyed pictures — my wife Alison has a distinct talent for and pre-occupation with oils — so an attempt at painting and drawing was appropriate to my family circumstances. Oil painting is particularly difficult: any amateur should have had some training, and of course, talent, if he or she is ever to produce present-able work. It also requires a considerable infrastructure of materials and besides takes an interminable time to set up and clear away at each session, or else demands a studio reserved for the purpose. Painting in oils accordingly seemed over-ambitious. Drawing in pencil or ink which calls for the simplest of materials offered a solution, second best no doubt, but preferable for someone lacking any sort of artistic train-ing but not short of enthusiasm. My needs are limited to a drawing pad and one of those super-efficient black ink pencils, such as 'fine point'. There is no need for an easel when one has a lap, or for the prior preparation of the canvas, no cleaning of brushes or palette. In fact no tiresome preliminaries to starting or stopping. My practice embraces economy of effort to a high degree. It is the application that's not so easy as my sketches will confirm. Drawing therefore it has so far been in my retirement. It's a matter of recognising one's limitations with an easy conscience.

As soon as I started I found how absorbing and satisfying this occupation can be. One's efforts have the same effect as one's offspring. They may not be perfect but they are one's own and they are personal creations that did not exist before. One's critical faculties are eroded but that's no great harm if one is to persist. To this extent, therefore, drawings met my original intention to furnish some material memorial to my short existence here on earth. A visit to the dusty shelves of any second hand bookshop however will soon disabuse one of the idea that authorship guarantees widespread immortality. Like many creative activities which, for most people, are no more than hobbies in a leisured age, there are far too many practi-tioners. Still one should never allow oneself to be discouraged by the competition, particularly when the outcome does not matter. That's one of the prime joys of retirement — you don't have to impress anyone superior or achieve any specified target — you are your own master.

Lightheartedly dismissing from my mind the competition as irrelevant to my plans, the first hurdle to present itself was the question of subject matter. This is extremely difficult. When unarmed with paper or pencil the countryside bursts with promise. Almost any view holds great possibility. Let one have a blank sheet of drawing paper and a pen at the ready and the promise evaporates. Virtually any view appears laden with difficulties and replete with reasons why that particular scene should not be attempted. Fortunately a solution to this first difficulty presented itself. It soon dawned on me that, in any view, when a church was visible, the church formed the focus of the picture. On the few occasions when the church was not the centre of attraction it appeared as an essential back-drop. I found that as I looked about, my eye was inevitably led to and held by the church. Perhaps living along-side one, as I now do, has had something to do with my predilection for ancient architecture of modest proportions.

Churches accordingly offered the answer to my problem of composition. But not any church; they have to be old, that's to say pre-Victorian, to appeal to me, the more isolated the better and certainly not in towns. Because in fact the great religious and church building periods ended with the Tudors, that means that my target churches are medieval. Happily Kent is blessed with an abundance of ancient, unassuming and remote country churches so what could be more convenient or agreeable for me?

An unwanted consequence of books and articles such as this, particularly those travel articles in the week-end papers drawing attention to beauty spots, can be that these eulogies tend to corrupt the places they extol. However, I should be very surprised, but gratified nevertheless, if my readership is anything but micro and the rare birds who inspect an isolated country church on my recommendation are unlikely to do any harm whatsoever. They might, on the contrary, put a small donation in the box for the upkeep of the fabric. The churches portrayed in this little book may safely continue to grow older and mellow in their solitude.

I don't know why these venerable country churches should exert such a fascina-tion. Perhaps it is something to do with romanticising over the medieval period in our history with its knights in armour, castles, battles and so on. For those who lived through them, the centuries after the Conquest can hardly have been com-fortable or secure; they cannot compare for creature comfort with the twentieth century, but the medieval populace has left behind memorials of astonishing and persistent beauty and which we, with all our technological ability, will do well to emulate in our turn. I cannot feel optimistic that the inhabitants in the year 2500 will gaze on any remaining works of 1980 with as much admiration as we give to those of 1280. Just for a moment look about you and consider what of all that we manufacture today can have any hope of a continued existence in 500 years' time. Very little, I fancy, except perhaps radio-active nuclear waste. In comparing the lasting qualities of our achievements with those of the twelfth century, we should, I suggest adopt a proper sense of humility.

3

When one reflects that these early masons cannot have enjoyed much in the way of formal education or architectural training, probably many were illiterate, it is even more remarkable what they achieved. Unlike today's designers, the builders of the Middle Ages, no doubt prompted by genuine religious convictions, must have invested a moral significance in their calling which would seem to have precluded any element of economy in construction. Thoroughness and time a-plenty were probably regarded as virtues and not obstacles. Every parish church, however poor the parish and however small the church, was thought of as God's house and, as we used to say in the Navy, was built to battleship standards. One should remember, I suppose, that something like 10%, possibly more, of the current gross domestic product, however that may be defined, went to the Church so there can have been no question of shortage of funds overall. Imagine what we could create now with 10% of today's resources. But since anything we plan in this paradise of planners follows Murphy's Law and invariably turns out contrary to intention, it could be that the twentieth century would be less successful than the earlier and less sophisticated age. At all events there can be no argument that we have been left permanent artifacts, dotted about the countryside, of astonishing beauty and unlikely, in a sceptical age, to be repeated. Leaving aside any religious aspect, they ought to be worth preserving and recording for their own sakes.

The preservation of such buildings, exotic in this secular age, presents, I feel, an insoluble problem. We simply are not prepared to allocate sufficient resources to their upkeep. There are many more than are needed for religious purposes and, to the non-communicant, the claims of say the national health service unarguably take precedence over those of redundant churches. As objects of historical significance and rural and local importance, responsibility for their well being can no longer fairly be said to reside solely with the clergy who, doubtless would do what they could if they had the money. But I cannot, for example, see the 'rates' or a central government committed to tax reduction, doing so either. As one of nature's pessimists, I can only envisage a continued deterioration of the fabric and neglect by parishioners. Presumably that is what happened to the abbeys and priories after the dissolution of the monasteries in Henry VIII's time and to the castles prior to that. Crumbling ruins are atmospheric and elegiac but we will all be the losers by the disappearance of even the humblest church. Selfishly, I can derive some comfort from the thought that it will not be my generation which will feel most loss; these churches were designed with a generous margin of structural strength and should withstand natural decay for a few hundred years yet.

Lest the reader should suspect that I am pleading a special case on behalf of what is now a minority in this country, I must acknowledge to being more agnostic than faithful. It is the church building, its surroundings and associations in which I am interested, not the theological doctrine it stands or stood for. I can't help feeling that, despite the teaching of western religion, it is a contradiction to claim that the Creator can be both omnipotent and benevolent. The history of mankind hardly bears out this theory. So my attachment to ancient, rural churches is almost entirely aesthetic. Very likely that is to my disadvantage but when faith is inadequate, the brain cannot be made to accept belief if it doesn't want to. To be flippant, if my agnosticism turns out to be misplaced, I will plead at the last trump that at least I enjoyed His churches and drew a great many of them.

Before further heresy is perpetrated, it may now be the place to describe how I set about my voyage of exploration. Bearing in mind my artistic shortcomings, I decided that lack of quality in my sketches would be mitigated to an extent by quantity and specialisation. In other words, I intended to concentrate exclusively on Kent and thereby hopefully amass a more complete and unified record. To be sure one single master work would be far superior to a hundred lesser sketches. But in the absence of the unattainable master work, the hundred lesser pieces might gain in authority from identity and cohesiveness. Rather like stamp collecting as I remember from my youth, concentration on a few countries generally gives a better result than taking the whole world as one's oyster. So think I, and living at Hadlow with all of Kent around me, Kent became my oyster to be prised open and its ecclesiastical pearls revealed — undiluted by the attractions of neighbouring counties.

Although it may sound so to a reader of these lines, I do not delude myself that I am the first to appreciate or record the beauties of the countryside churches. The reference shelves of any good public library are well stocked with dusty, mostly unregarded volumes of this category; excellent they invariably are and models of learning and detail. I am not presumptuous enough to hope to emulate these fore-runners in quality or expect to be regarded any more, or even as much as they are. Nevertheless, the effort is rewarding in itself and, as remarked earlier, my own.

Armed with a map and the erudite Pevsner's Buildings of England, Kent Sections, and the use of the family car, I can go straight to my target with no time-consuming or frustrating prospecting around. The choice of church to sketch was based on nothing more profound than distance and the first church I drew was to all intents and purposes the nearest. Now, after over a hundred excursions, I am obliged to venture further. It means more driving but one does get to know one's county to a degree one might not otherwise achieve. I am fortunate that, on the whole, Kent is so unspoilt and rural. At times I feel rather like a twenteth century Lambarde, but how his lengthy perambulations were accomplished without benefit of a motor car I cannot imagine. One is full of admiration for those pilgrims of a pre-automotive age.

It is not very easy to describe the pleasure one experiences on arriving at some country church. Provided it's not the week-end, there is rarely anyone about and that's a bonus. What houses there are in the vicinity are generally attractive in their own right and they and the church both gain from their proximity. The churchyard is always evocative, full of mellowed tombstones in various stages of disarray, venerable yews that one imagines are veterans of Agincourt and dominating all is the centuries-old church. Most of the inscriptions on the headstones or plinths are indecipherable so that these earlier attempts at immortality have been frustrated by the passage of time. Some of our forebears must have had a fairly substantial conceit of their own importance to judge by the more elaborate or grandiose memorials. But it can only have been a tiny fraction of those who have lived who are so recorded. The modern practice of cremation, though presumably more hygienic, will ensure regrettably that there will be few more such stone ornaments for later generations to admire (and decipher). I think perhaps now that, if parishes were to list annually the great events of their parish and enter these records year by year in the church or churchyard, a more certain communal immortality would be obtained than can be achieved by individual monuments, charming and nostalgic though many of them may be. In these more egalitarian days the communal approach might be more appropriate.

At all events I have found that the church and its memorials instantly transport one from the 20th century to a bygone age. It is remarkable how often in practically any church however unpretentious, one finds some reminder or confirmation of the history one learnt at school or has since read about. Most churches, if they are unlocked, not always the case by any means, and understandably so, contain a brief historical chronicle of the church and its prominent monuments. This little booklet is a great help in appreciating what one is looking at. Equally, I find that the enthusiastic Arthur Mee's excellent volume on Kent an invaluable source of local information and pride.

It must by now be obvious that my account does not pretend to guide book status or claim any architectural or ecclesiastical authority (and certainly it is not written for the expert). Many distinctive characteristics of the churches depicted will be omitted, not intentionally but by error, and here and there unique features will have been overlooked — or indeed avoided because they are difficult to draw. Since my drawings do, nevertheless, display these country churches as they have been perceived in the early 1980s, a visitor to the undisturbed shelves of a second-hand bookshop (so unflatteringly commented on previously) in say the year 2080 might find something to stimulate his or her antiquarian interest. The visitor might indeed be a descendant of mine, I would like to think so, and the date might be 2180, not as removed in future times as the subjects of this volume.

I hope that the sketches which follow and their accompanying comment will go some way towards conveying why I have so much enjoyed my voyage of exploration into one aspect of Kent. May others who are now retired or are uneasily contemplating the long silences of retirement take heart and be equally fortunate in their turn.

Hadlow 1984

BOUGHTON MALHERBE
St. Nicholas

Manor granted to Robert de Malherbe

This is the small grey ragstone church, largely Decorated in style, that constitutes the eastern finial of the line of seven churches along the Wealden ridge that leads to Lenham. Its parish is scattered and its only immediate neighbours are the Tudor mansion, Boughton Place, and the one-time Victorian village schoolhouse.

To judge from the memorials the church was not always buried in obscurity and cow parsley; now it is far from the great world and more given to gathering moss than attracting attention. Its unexpected distinction derives from the Elizabethan family of Wotton of Boughton Place. One of these Wottons, it was, who coined that memorable definition of an ambassador:

An ambassador is an honest man
Sent to lie abroad for the good of his country.

As an ambassador for Elizabeth I he should have known. Apparently she paid him a visit at Boughton Malberbe and, so it is said, planted a yew to record the occasion. One can still see it today, full of life, in a nearby field protected by a brick and ragstone wall. It would be nice to claim that the yew which I have drawn by the tower is the royal yew but that would be taking too much of a liberty with the truth — and lese-majeste to boot.

Fortunately two ladies turned up while I was sketching and I was able to inspect the interior for the first time. It is compact but there is much of interest; the restrained Wotton brasses, the more flamboyant coats of arms of the Akers-Douglas family, an elegant 'cabinet makers' font canopy, three recumbent marble lions from a vanished monument, finely carved bench ends in the choir stalls, a perilous-looking ladder doing duty for a staircase to the bell chamber and two memorials to past priests which I could not resist. The first, that of Dr Lionell Sharpe (deceased 1630) recorded that he was:

Chaplaine to the Earle of Essex
Then to Queene Elizabeth at her own choyse
Prince Henry and King James

One must acknowledge that the Rev. Sharpe moved in the best circles in his time but doubtless the position had its perils as well as its privileges. The second was a ledger slab commemorating the Rev. Stanhope (deceased 1720) who for fifty years was both rector of Boughton Malherbe and Great Langton in distant Yorkshire, the latter by dispensation of Charles II. It would be disrespectful to speculate which parish considered itself the more favoured.

Boughton Malherbe provided an unexpected experience. Alone in the church, I was startled to find myself face to face with a flower-laden coffin in the aisle. Impossible to feel sadness for the departed; what better place to spend ones last few hours above ground than in solitary state in the peace of St. Nicholas, Boughton Malherbe. I hope I may be as fortunate in my turn.

ULCOMBE
All Saints

Owl valley

Closely sandwiched between East Sutton and Boughton Malherbe on the ridge of high ground that runs west from Lenham towards Maidstone, Ulcombe church enjoys a commanding position overlooking the Weald. If one stands in the church-yard facing south the prospect is quite magnificent; an unbroken sea of green recedes to the distant horizon and the forest clearance looks as if it never happened. Before the Normans came to build their church, the low Weald consisted of the vast trackless forest of Anderida and from the church the landscape must seem little changed today despite a lapse of a thousand years. One can understand why a string of village churches was built on the ridge; the tangled prehistoric forest resisting clearance by human muscle and primitive implements until eventually economic forces in the shape of a demand for timber for charcoal to smelt the local iron ore provided the necessary impetus. Being difficult, and possibly dangerous, to penetrate, the forest no doubt offered a more reliable sanctuary to those who had offended the Norman establishment than did the seven churches on the high ground above.

The church justifies its situation. The present building is of 13th and 14th century construction embodying remnants of the earlier Norman work; although restored in 1870 the rubble ragstone, happily spared the prudent Victorian repointing, still retains its bloom of crumbling antiquity. It is difficult to draw for topographical reasons and no view that I have seen allows one to show satisfactorily the typical Kent tower silhouetted against the skyline which is how one would like to picture it. One must content oneself, as I have, with a glimpse of the tower, no more than one of the Decorated south windows and, inevitably, the two giant guardian yews which flank the approach to the porch.

Inside, the church is a surprise. Someone has imaginatively cleared away all un-necessary clutter and covered the exposed walls with whitewash. So described, this decor hardly sounds sufficiently mysterious for a religious building but, in fact, an emphatic impression of space is thus created and the aspects of importance in the church are, as a result, more clearly revealed. Essentially these consist of faded fragments of wall paintings, three table tombs against the north wall and the two generous and well-preserved 15th century Maydestone and Sentleger brasses. In contrast but in no way conflicting with austere medieval atmosphere is the modern pulpit, a skeletal framework of iron, and the altar in the south chapel, a brickwork construction. I don't know what altars are normally made of but bonded brickwork is, I fancy, something of a rarity.

At the risk of seeming patronising, I must congratulate whoever is responsible for the present state of the interior of Ulcombe church; it is admirably suited to its age and situation.

This is the next, and third, church westwards on the ragstone ridge running from Lenham. Observing that Ulcombe is only one mile to the east and Sutton Valence one-and-a-half miles to the west, the ridge does seem to have been somewhat over-churched. We can be grateful for such extravagance, however.

East Sutton gives me the chance to show off, a habit I can rarely resist. That morning, with my early morning tea, I had been struggling with Bertrand Russell's 'History of Western Philosophy' and had reached the point where Russell introduces his reader to Sir Robert Filmer whose work in 1680 the 'Natural Power of Kings' defended the doctrine of the divine right of kings. Imagine therefore my surprised delight to find that the leading historical family associated with East Sutton was that of the Filmers' and that Sir Robert is duly immortalised therein. Bertrand Russell relates that the Filmers' house, Sutton Park, which stands on the lip of the ridge immediately below the church, was plundered ten times by the Parliamentarians, presumably because of the owners' Royalist sympathies. Sutton Park has withstood these depredations without permanent damage.

The church was locked but the key could be obtained from the house. As Sutton Park looked every bit as interesting as the church I set off for the key. The park looked immaculate if severe and a forbidding notice forbade photography. I wondered if my sketching came under a similar interdict.

At the front door another notice told me curtly to ring and wait. In time a crushed-looking girl arrived to fetch the key and claim it on my return. The explanation for this bleak air is that Sutton Park is now a girls' borstal. It seems a sad come-down from the divine right of kings or from the 83rd Field Regiment R.A. who trained there before crossing to Normandy in 1944.

The tower in my drawing, which was added in 1420, is Perpendicular as is the south porch to the right. Apparently the church stands on the site of a wooden thatched Saxon church which is recorded in the Domesday Book. After the Conquest, the manor of East Sutton was granted to Bishop Odo of Baueux who must have been a most acquisitive man notwithstanding his assumed Christian pretensions. The oak door of the porch bears bullet marks from the Civil War so both church and house have been in the wars, but survived nevertheless to continue to grace the ragstone ridge.

Shoreham stands in the Darent valley and, indeed the river Darent runs under the village street. Its claim to fame for some rests on its association with the now-fashionable painter Samuel Palmer and his artistic friends, nick-named the 'Ancients' who practised in the village about 1830. Their style was romantic and idealistic and their feelings can only have been nourished by such an idyllic setting. Actually, I don't particularly care for Palmer's style but that could be said to be my misfortune and to show my lack of judgement.

Shoreham is an extremely picturesque village which in no way disgraces the church standing in its midst. The whole neighbourhood is remarkably unspoilt and distinguished for somewhere so near to London. But not for much longer. As I understand the situation, planning permission has been granted to drive a motorway through the valley but with what necessity escapes me; we enjoy (if that's the right word) a super-abundance of motorways in the county. Around Maidstone, not far from the entrance to the Darent valley, one finds (or in my case is confused by) a glut of motorways running parallel to each other and separated by a mere mile or two. I am not anti-motorway in principle; indeed I think they often add aesthetic value to the countryside and do quarantine through traffic from the rest of us. But enough is often more than enough and for Shoreham's sake one might have looked to OPEC and the price of petrol for salvation.*

Shoreham church is of a later period than most I have drawn. In fact, the tower I show dates from 1775 which my church reference book declares to be Hanoverian and is the last of the architectural styles to be dignified as a period. Presumably in ecclesiastical taxonomy, the Victorian and modern times do not count. I quite agree.

When I made my sketch, it was February and bitterly cold. Fortunately, I drew from a bench outside the George Inn and was able, before rigor mortis set in, to restore my circulation (and artistic morale) within. I was not entirely happy with the drawing, (in truth, not happy at all) and am sure that Samuel Palmer and his 'Ancients' would agree.

* My understanding was correct. Now in the summer of 1984, the construction of the M25 through the Darent valley is in full spate — fortunately well away from the village along the opposing slope. Nevertheless I expect that the roar of the traffic will one day contend discordantly with the sound of the organ in the church.

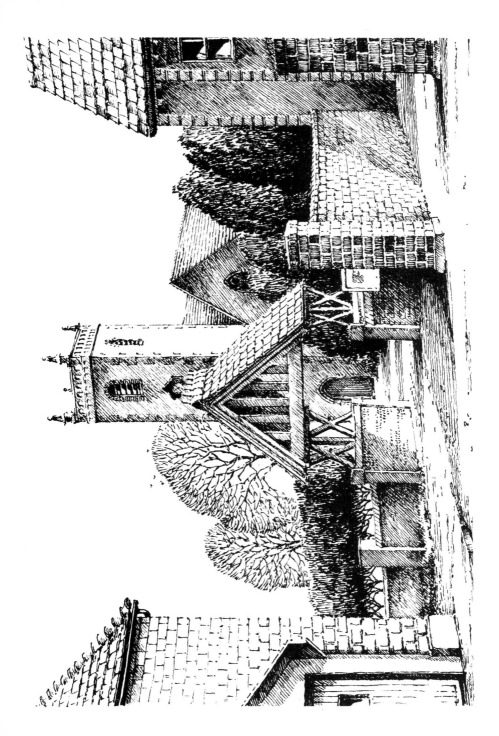

I was delighted to include Seal church in my sketching odyssey although I am not entirely sure that it still qualifies as a country church. Once it did, indeed it was no more than part of the parish of Kemsing, but today it is more likely to become a suburb of Sevenoaks.

Years ago, when travelling by train from Maidstone to Victoria my attention was excited by the sight of an apparently lonely church standing proudly on the skyline to the south, and I wished I could have been there rather than a passenger of British Rail. The identity of this prominent church remained unknown until the occasion of this sketch. Even, after the conventional approach from the village I remained unaware of my prize until viewed from the northern slope of the churchyard. And there was my sought-after railway church. Close inspection in no way detracted from memory.

In many church sketches, the foreground poses more problems than the building itself. If one is too close the perspective can be distorted; too far away and the view may be obstructed or a dull expanse presents itself and spoils the effect. Here at Seal, seen from the south, I have been able to include the handsome Tudor tower, the long, undulating keel-like ridge of the 13th century south aisle, the jumbled patchwork of headstones saving the foreground and a suggestion of the regimented double line of yews marching on the porch from the lych gate.

A reproduction of a print in the British Museum in the illustrated pamphlet of the church shows that in the 1890s, the octagonal stair turret was capped by a mini parapet spire. Not so in my sketch of the 1980s. A curiosity that has struck me when examining old prints of churches is the often bare and treeless aspect of the churchyards. For instance there is no sign of the disciplined column of yews and not many tombstones either at Seal in 1890. Today these yews are splendid and compete on equal terms with the claims of the building. Although it makes for difficulty in composition, I much prefer to see a country church surrounded and protected by aged yews and weeping ashes.

Surprising for a church in so dominating a position and with such a fortress-like tower, Seal has led a placid and tranquil life in the centuries since its Norman foundation. One hopes that this happy state of affairs will long continue and that Seal village and its church will not be entirely engulfed in the rising tide of twentieth century materialism from Sevenoaks.

HALLING
St. John the Baptist

Hall dwellers

Pevsner is not prepared to allocate more than a few column inches of his scholarship to Halling. I can understand why. The church stands immediately upon the heavily industrialised road that runs along the north bank of the Medway to Stroud. Nowadays, the whole area lies under a coating of grey dust from the huge cement works downstream. It cannot always have been thus.

My interest in Halling is more personal. It was the summer residence of Hamo, Bishop of Rochester in the 1320s and vestiges of the palace are still visible beyond the churchyard wall. Hamo is my favourite bishop, not for any religious piety or ecclesiastical fame which he may have displayed or enjoyed but because of a remote and tenuous ancestral relationship. It was not easy for Hamo to secure his mitre. Much lobbying was necessary, in this country and on the continent, in competition with Queen Isabella and her confessor, the rival contender. Happily, Hamo got the job, perhaps because both queen and confessor were French. Once enthroned, Hamo seems to have led a withdrawn life, sustained by diplomatic illness at moments of particular danger. In the modern jargon, he kept a low profile; wisely in such a turbulent age. He was, though, careful to follow convention and place his relatives in such rewarding sinecures as First Sergeant of the Brewery at the Cathedral, ditto at the Priory, and a lesser individual as Second Sergeant of the Laundry. Such appointments may not sound too grand today but I would imagine that these positions were once not to be sneezed at. On one occasion at Halling, Hamo lost thirty two members of his household to the plague but escaped himself; a circumstance which exhibits a proper respect for the privileges of rank, I think.

The Medway flows close east of the ruins of the bishop's palace. It must have been lovely in his day; I believe that they even grew vines there. I tried to penetrate beyond the brambles and nettles to the river only to retire in some confusion from a gypsy encampment and its guardian mongrels. Another manifestation of the blight of twentieth century 'progress' on the rural simplicities of the past.

So far as the church is concerned, I will emulate Pevsner and let my sketch speak for me. To an extent though, its unusual framework clock on the four faces of the pyramid cap on top of the tower (not too clear in my sketch) must raise an eyebrow or two from passers-by. As remarked elsewhere in this book, clockwork mechanisms on medieval towers are out of place and unnecessary today. They can only be justified, perhaps as at Halling, if they attract the attention that would otherwise ignore the church.

But for Hamo, I fear it would no longer qualify as a countryside church.

CHARING
St. Peter and St. Paul

Ceorra's people

Charing was a settlement in Saxon times, sheltering below the downs from the east winds, and it was probably used as a stopping place by pilgrims on their way to Canterbury. The land on which the church stands was given to St. Augustine about 600 AD. No doubt about the same time, the manor of Charing became part of the Archdiocese of Canterbury. So as a human settlement it has more than a millenium of recorded history and Christian religion under its belt.

The church has had an eventful history being disastrously burnt at the end of the 16th century leaving virtually only the tower and walls standing. One would not realise that today, and with its fine strong west tower and well-maintained flint walls, the church has an air of undefeated permanence. There is, moreover, a remarkable tradition attached to Charing. Legend has it that the stone on which St. John the Baptist (and others too) were beheaded was brought to England after one of the Crusades and presented to the church in the reign of either Richard I or Richard II. It is supposed that the stone was built into one of the altars or used as a marker but now there is no trace of it — perhaps the fire was the occasion for its disappearance. At any rate, in 1936 the then Vicar could assert with confidence that if Charing church should ever be subjected to the rigour of excavation suffered by the Pharaohs in their tombs the stone would be uncovered and identified. I wish I could share the vicar's confidence but I dare say that Charing's peace is better preserved by its absence.

In the 15th and 16th centuries Charing was a popular archiepiscopal residence but in 1520 Archbishop Warham was sufficiently incautious, probably he had little alternative, to provide accommodation in the palace to Henry VIII and his substantial retinue as they made their way through Kent via Otford, Leeds and Charing to the Field of the Cloth of Gold in France. The Archbishop's hospitality suffered the usual consequences from Henry and the manor was duly sequestrated from Warham's successor, the unfortunate Cranmer. The ruin on the left of my sketch is what remains of the gateway of the Archbishop's palace — what other village church displays so singular an approach?

One cannot comment on Charing church and omit its village which is correspondingly attractive at the centre. It lies, tight-knit, at the junction of two important roads but has been saved from the traffic by strategically placed by-passes. Indeed the fleeting motorist need hardly be aware of this gem of a village; he is too preoccupied, or should be, to spare a glance at the tumble of tiled roofs and the beckoning church tower. Modern pilgrims have 20th century needs and different destinations from their medieval predecessors and the motel a mile or two up the road is more likely to claim their attention than the peaceful church. Good.

COWDEN
St. Mary Magdalene

Cowden church occupies the far south-west corner of my Kent parish. The village, something of a beauty spot, has an air of Sussex and its historical association with iron smelting reinforces the impression. There is still a practising smithy in the village (1981) but the prices they ask for their work must restrict their clientele, I suspect, to those with well-filled purses. My pocket was not disturbed.

The church has a less permanent appearance than the more orthodox Kent churches I have drawn. I think this is conveyed by the needle spire, which together with the tower, is clothed entirely in wooden shingles. In fact the church has been there since the late 13th century; its air of impermanence is thus out by at least 500 years. One should not judge by appearances, they say, but in most cases, they neglect to say what it is one should judge by. So appearance is always important, if occasionally misleading. The wooden steeple does dominate the little church; steeples and spires, particularly those that emerge from broaches (ie the conversion of four planes into eight, I think is correct) are not easy to draw without distortion. I have at last realised, after many distortions, that from whatever angle or however many planes there are, the apex must be centred or the whole structure will appear eccentric. This realisation has, I hope, eliminated some of my grosser misdrawings.

This drawing is my second attempt at Cowden. On the first occasion I established myself in the long grass outside the churchyard to the east. The rampant vegetation which surrounded me there sent me later to my book of wild flowers for enlightenment. I thought, I dare say wrongly, that I recognised Broad Dock — good for nettle stings and for keeping butter cool; Tormentil — aptly named as it was used in milk for dosing children suffering from diarrhoea (or so my book says); and Vipers' Buglos — good for bees and butterflies but no mention of vipers. Sad to say the medicinal herbs got the better of my pen and so I have reluctantly returned to a more conventional, if less interesting, rendering of an attractive and much older church than it appears at first glance. I think, after ruminating about my defeat by Vipers' Buglos etc, that a short course in botanical drawing might simplify composition and could contribute to the foreground improvement of my sketches. The course though will have to wait for volume II if there is to be one.

Pace Arthur Mee, Tonge is no longer the prettiest part of Kent. It may have been in 1936 when he wrote his famous book, although I doubt it, but it suffers from the encroachment of the least lovely parts of Sittingbourne. Today, the church's immediate surroundings consist of a row of four council-type cottages and, across the road, a dump for derelict cars. Despite these ubiquitous specimens of the motor age, the church has a simple, lonely grandeur and I found it very striking. Once, as it stood solidly rising above the Swale marshes it must have conveyed an air of authority and safe refuge.

Not far away is the earthen mound of an ancient castle. Legend has it that it was here that King Vortigern swapped his kingdom for the hand of Rowena, daughter of the invader, Hengist. There was also some clever stuff with ox hides, but I find both legends hard to credit. Surely any kingdom worth the name would contain more than enough (equivalent) Rowenas for any king. Also I would be disappointed if the Royal Navy would have named one of its V and W class destroyers after a king known to have displayed such impulsive and irresponsible qualities.

The church was locked but the key could be had from one of the cottages — named St. Giles Houses after the church no doubt. Thither I went to find a pensioner pottering about his vegetable garden. Armed with the key, I returned to the church followed hot foot by the old man, older man, I should say — in case I should make off with the candlesticks was my first unkind thought. Not so. The church had become the old man and his wife's raison d'etre and pride and joy. He took me round the interior at length explaining its finer points. It was a most enjoyable and unexpected experience. His wife did the flowers, and although I think it was mid-week, there was not a dead head or unwatered vase to be seen. I seem to remember one curiosity of the interior; although Pevsner makes no mention, one or more of the tower buttresses intruded upon the nave as if the tower had been built first with the nave added round it later. I am sure that can't be the correct sequence.

As with the church and its volunteer guardians, I was happy with my drawing on this occasion. It proclaims the strong simplicity of the Early English tower and just manages to suggest the huge nave roof reaching down almost to ground level without permitting the slightest evidence of anything later than say 1500. One can almost hear the Anglo-Saxon invaders marching up the roadway and the tower, if it was standing then, would offer ready and reliable asylum.

St. Peter and St. Paul

Borden, which lies just over one mile south-west of Sittingbourne, in fact about the same distance away as Tonge is to the eastward, has escaped unblemished. Approach from the west and you are unaware of the existence of Sittingbourne; approach from Sittingbourne and it is as if an invisible curtain separates the two. Magical really and I can only surmise that ownership of a belt of land has acted as a sort of 'cordon sanitaire'. Preservation of the countryside from the blight of urban spread is one of the benefits for which large-scale landowners are rarely given credit. It is an unplanned and unconscious act of fortune wholly beneficial in its effects and more effective than are green belts which are often despoiled with the approval of officialdom.

Borden has a grand village church. The tower is Norman and of sufficient dimensions to manage without buttresses. At the west foot of the tower is a distinctive arched Norman doorway embellished with zigzags and a fish-scale pattern and supported by six columns. When I drew the church, I was too taken with the pillar monument in the foreground to notice that I had obscured the west door. Actually the pillar monument is also very fine and I can't regret its inclusion.

In fact, I enjoy drawing headstones as much as anything. They do contribute to the general atmosphere of past generations watching over their church and the village, and those churchyards which lack a sufficiency suffer thereby. In this respect, the practice, if it is a practice of the church, to uproot headstones and line them up against a wall is to be deplored. I don't in contrast much like modern tombstones which have had insufficient time to weather and gather moss. One gets no pleasure from a municipal cemetery and I wonder why there should be such a difference in experience.

I must do some research into churchyards and their organisation. Presumably there is some sort of hierarchy of site; along the path to the porch or under the east wall of the chancel being premium spots perhaps. Inside the church no doubt ranks above the churchyard, the chancel above the nave, the aisle above under the pews and so on.

It can be a depressing subject to some people and when I attempt to discuss our possible resting places, my wife gets fairly short-tempered with me. One should always look facts in the eye, I maintain, and try to avoid being surprised by the inevitable.

BREDHURST
St. Peter

To judge from the state of the churchyard, where the grass was rougher, and wetter, than I have met before, St. Peter's, Bredhurst, must be verging on a state of redundancy. I managed to coincide, though, with one of its bursts of activity; as I sketched inconspicuously from the long grass behind a row of tombstones there was a constant important coming and going in preparation for a wedding. At the start the church was locked and a small girl — to be one of the choir — offered to fetch the key and unlock but in the circumstances developing, I also would have become redundant, not to say superfluous, if caught inspecting the interior as the wedding party arrived. So I declined the offer but don't believe I missed too much. It was kind of the small girl though.*

Pevsner has little to say and likewise Arthur Mee possible because, like me, they regret the lost antiquity overlaid by Victorian restoration. This is a downland church of which there are many more than is required by the present community and from which one might infer more numerous, more religious and richer rural congregations in the past. The forgotten solitude of these withdrawn churches is part of their fascination for me and is what converts my wanderings into an exploration. They are certainly not always easy to find.

I sketched Bredhurst in the early summer. It is a delightful season to be about the countryside but there are drawbacks to too much time spent in this way. At home the grass is growing visibly, the weeds are rampant and ensuring their future, and the seed packets are clamorous for attention. One is constantly rebuked by the passing weeks; things in the garden left undone will never be done that year and one can spend the winter regretting one's lack of timely application. Similarly DIY; in an old house like mine, every window demands a surgical operation prior to painting. As we all know, postponement here guarantees more trouble later.

I tell myself that my churches have been where they are for a century or two and can very well wait while I sow my seeds. But the seeds are not important and the churches are and one's life is not limitless. So the churches will win but so, I am afraid, will the weeds.

* A subsequent visit the following spring, while the church was open for a gathering of flower ladies, confirmed my original estimate about the lack of points of interest but contradicted my observation on possible redundancy. Although hidden away from the village this little flint church, combining 13th and 19th century ecclesiastical architecture, is still very much alive and, to my knowledge, fondly regarded by its flower arrangers.

Headcorn is a very handsome wealden village with a correspondingly handsome church in an equally distinguished setting at the head of the wide village street. There the church stands with its strong square tower and its Perpendicular chancel and chapel windows framed by the avenue of horse chestnuts which were planted to celebrate Queen Victoria's diamond jubilee — lucky Headcorn that they were not elms.

However, although I would not dream of disparaging the architecture and contents of such a fine church as this, it is the trees, or rather one, that captures the imagination here. Well named by the Saxons, Headcorn is situated in that part of the Weald once covered by the great prehistoric forest of Anderida — now long since vanished. One survivor remains, though, to bear witness to a blanket of impenetrable woodland. There it rests, by the parvenu south porch, a majestic ruin of a noble oak.

What one sees today in this relic of the past is no more than a hollow, shattered shell, supported by wooden posts and stayed by steel wire rope, but refusing to die. Its ravaged trunk must be some ten feet in diameter, say thirty feet in girth, with its younger branches flowering and bursting with fresh green leaves when I sketched. That this methuselah is still growing vigorously was demonstrated to me by the owner of the cottage on the grounds of which I sat. Apparently, when he came to Headcorn, about forty years ago, the iron railings of the churchyard were quite clear of the tree — now they are embedded. Similarly, thirty years ago, the son of my informant pressed a clay tile into the bark — now the tile has been almost completely absorbed. Through owning the ground on which the tree partly stands, my new acquaintance can justly claim to share ownership with the church of what must be one of the oldest living trees in England. Fortunate man to enjoy such an unique possession.

So, notwithstanding that one must describe this church as a near perfect specimen of late 14th century ecclesiastic architecture, beautifully placed in its period village, one cannot help but find the Anderida oak more arresting. There are other churches in Kent just as magisterial with just as fine a set of Perpendicular windows or with as well preserved a medieval screen and so on but they don't have such a virile old patriarch to keep them company. My Headcorn friend proposes to recover an acorn and plant it; what a triumph to have an offspring when one is over a thousand years old. I hope the experiment is successful.

St. Botolph's is one of those churches which gain by their proximity to a great house and by association with its occupants. In this case, the house is Chevening Park, a mid seventeenth century house, of which the most famous and enduring owners have been the Stanhope family. I am not certain when the Stanhope family relinquished the house, fairly recently I fancy, and after considerable refurbishment, it was offered by its Trustees to the Prime Minister of the day for disposal as a sort of grace and favour house of 10 Downing Street. Prince Charles was the first beneficiary but I think the Foreign Secretary now (1982) has the use of the place. I cannot be sure because of the reluctance of the Chevening Estate Office to answer their telephone when I rang to check. No doubt they are pestered by cranks like me and their telephone is a source of annoyance.

To revert to St. Botolph's. It stands on the east side of the lane leading to the entrance to the Park. On the other side are what were once estate houses and a very attractive group they make. There is nothing else in the way of a village at Chevening and it is now effectively cut off from the world by the Downs above and the M25 below to the south. One can conclude, with confidence I feel, that in the heyday of the Stanhopes and their predecessors, the Lennards, the church was virtually their private chapel as there never has been much of a settlement at Chevening.

The church dates from the thirteenth century with traces in stone of an earlier building and is mainly Perpendicular in style. As a consequence of its connection with the once powerful Stanhopes the interior is of more interest than the exterior which is of conventional good taste but apart from exhibiting a fine example of galleting, not remarkable. It is the south (Stanhope) chapel with its memorials to members of the Stanhopes and the Lennards which attracts the attention and earns the comments of descriptive literature. My attention, though, was captured by one of those bequest boards in the tower base; this proclaimed, in gold lettering, that, in 1724, Lucy, Countess of Stanhope, provided a legacy of £1000 '. . . to be laid out in the purchase of South Sea Annuities, the interest of which is to be applied . . .' I can't see the authorities of today investing church monies in such an optimistically speculative venture as the South Sea Bubble and I fear that the churchgoing tenants can have seen little interest from the well-meant bequest.

One wonders who now attends the church other than the occasional idle visitor but the whole place was neat and tidy, church opened, grass being cut and so on when I was there. Very likely that is due to the influence of the great house which can hardly let its illustrious tenant and his important official guests worship in a run-down or neglected private chapel. Today the church must be something of an anachronism; one regrets the passing of its heyday and cannot but feel that, although the fabric will endure, it has reached the long autumn of its life. If Prince Charles had remained the tenant, the house and church might yet have enjoyed a life of greater consequence than even the Stanhopes could provide.

St. Peter and St. Paul

This version of St. Peter and St. Paul is my second attempt. The first took place early in my exploration of Kent's country churches when I was less practised and the original drawing, I felt, never did justice to this church. My second visit was made under extreme conditions; it was during that Whit week-end in 1984 described as 'the coldest and wettest Spring Bank Holiday for more than forty years'. I did, however, learn two things from sketching in the rain; one, that ink will not transfer from pen to paper when the latter is damp (I don't know why not) and two, that one can complete a perfectly serviceable rough sketch while holding aloft an open umbrella.

Despite the rain, the church was unexpectedly unlocked. Inside I was rewarded by a copy of the church's excellent and knowledgeable brochure by John Newman. I imagine that the author is the same John Newman who wrote the two authoritative volumes of Pevsner's 'Buildings of England' that concern Kent and so the quality of the brochure is not surprising. Armed with this pamphlet I began my circuit of the interior only to find that I had disturbed a courting couple in the chancel. There is quite a lot to see in this church and, as I scrutinised the memorials and the architectural mouldings, I could not avoid a sensation of unspoken messages telling me to be gone. And so I did but not before I had time to admire the ledger stones that entirely floor the Lady Chapel. These all relate to one family and run from 1683 to 1799 and, in their modest way, although in the context of Ash not modest at all, put one in mind of the celebrated Cobham brasses on the chancel floor at Cobham.

Externally the church is most attractive. It appears to have been rebuilt of flint, from an earlier building, in the 13th and 15th centuries. There must have been a near disaster in the 18th century which called for the replacement of the flint by Georgian brickwork in the upper story of the tower and in the complete stair turret together with iron tie-bars lower down in the tower. This mixture of bricks and mottled flint produces a most vivid effect, the square tower in particular holding the eye and quickening the imagination.

When I first went to Ash, with my wife and dog and sketching pad, we had recently returned from a visit to Somerset. One cannot be in Somerset without admiring the village churches with their elaborate and magnificent towers. Compared with Kent, Somerset towers have the edge and, since they are mainly perpendicular, are of a later date. They could afford to be so grand then. It was the explosion of the sheep and wool industry which created the all-important surplus over consumption to finance those ambitious West Country churches. Today we spend our capital surplus in supporting the improvident nationalised industries and I shall forbear to comment on that.

Wickhambreux lies on the little Stour, one of a group of ancient villages a few miles east of Canterbury. It is a far cry from Hadlow but well worth the journey. The old 'Breux' part of its name was added to Wickham when a William de Breuse owned the manor in 1285. The village has now been designated a conservation area and it does present a timeless picture with the 14th century church, manor, inn and mill encircling the village green.

The church makes a good solid appearance of square, unfussy tower and Perpendicular windows. The east window in the chancel was restored at the turn of this century with fresh art-nouveau stained glass from New York commissioned for it. It looks very fine in my drawing.

Arthur Mee, generally so reliable when it comes to gossip about the places he describes, seems to have slept when he came to Wickhambreux. It is the unremarked female inhabitants who steal the show here. The first in time to excite the imagination was Rosamund Clifford who lived just by the church gate in the manor, Wickhambreux Court. Rosamund, otherwise the 'Fair Rosamund', had I believe two illegitimate children by the youthful Henry II to be. She cannot have profited greatly from her liaison as Henry was married officially shortly afterwards to Eleanor of Aquitane leaving Rosamund to retire to end her days in a nunnery at Godstow outside Oxford. When my wife and I visited Oxford to see our son, we made a pilgrimage to Godstow but nothing now remains except a few sad stones under the austere care of the Ministry of Works. No sign of the Fair Rosamund's resting place.

A comparable, if more conventional, successor to Rosamund at the manor was Joan Plantagenet who married the Black Prince and gave birth to the future Richard II. He it was who dealt so summarily with Wat Tyler and the revolting peasants from Kent. Probably not a few from Wickhambreux suffered at the hands of his judges.

The third lady to arouse the historian was the widow of Joan Plantagenet's brother, the Earl of Kent. After his death, the widow entered a convent only to scandalise everyone by coming clandestinely to Wickhambreux to marry a prominent warrior knight. Not the sort of thing nuns were supposed to do, particularly those close to the crown.

Despite therefore, its present air of innocence, Wickhambreux has clearly had its ration of the old Adam and Eve and one wonders what view the church and its incumbents took of the goings on. If they were wise, they looked the other way.

EGERTON
St. James

Ecgheard's farmstead

If Egerton church can make no claim to illustrious or even infamous, associations in the past and, so far as I know having been denied entrance on two occasions by the locked door, exhibits no monuments of sufficient merit to arouse learned comment, at least it makes amends by an unusually splendid tower. I have sketched the church twice — the first time from the east, the second from the west. The view from the east mistakenly allows a luxuriant blackberry bush to monopolise the foreground at the expense of the church; in the view from the west, which you see here, I have had the sense to eschew irrelevancies and let the tower speak for itself. It really is spectacular and one would like to know what can have been in the minds of the builders who decided in the 1460s to grace a minor hilltop hamlet with such a major soaring structure.

Perched on its eminence above the sunken road, the tower can arouse doubts concerning stability. When I began to write about my church drawings, my son who read engineering at Oxford insisted on my reading one of his paperbacks on structures to minimise my more egregious mistakes and displays of ignorance. I don't know that he will be successful in this.

It appears that walls are subject to two forces; one vertically downwards caused by the weight of its own masonry and a second, diagonally off the vertical, to a greater or lesser degree, caused by the sideways push of the roof which the wall supports. According to the theory of the parallelogram of forces (which bored one so at school) these two forces can theoretically be resolved into one force in a downwards but not exactly vertical direction. If this direction takes the resultant force outside the surface of the wall, the wall falls down. However the architect can either increase the downward component to bring the resolved force closer to the vertical by adding weight at the top, in the form of a pinnacle, say, or place buttresses at strategic intervals in order to keep the combined thrust inside the widened surface of the wall. In Kent, builders have favoured buttresses and there are few pinnacles to be seen. My sketch shows that Egerton has the English arrangement of paired buttresses against the tower and these reach 'unusually high via many set-offs' says Pevsner.

It is not clear to me why the tower, with no roof to give a sideways thrust and with a very substantial downwards pressure caused by the mass of the masonry, should need such elaborate and sturdy buttresses. In Hadlow, our Saxo-Norman tower is handsomely stabilised by two solid buttresses but the Victorian chapel, which has a roof and hence a sideways thrust on its walls and faces our garden, has none. Somebody must be wrong. I think I had better have a word with the vicar to explain these mysteries to him and suggest that he goes easy on the fortissimo hymns. Egerton need have no such worries.

ASHURST
St. Martin of Tours

Ash wooded hills

Another small church on the south west boundary of my parish. Indeed it has far more an appearance of Sussex than of Kent. The church stands above the busy A264 surrounded by beech trees and must be largely invisible to and ignored by the passing traffic. So much the better, I am sure it would say if it could speak.

I don't know the age of this church; the porch is dated 1621 but I would suppose from the window in the nave that it is 14th to 15th century. My uncertainty stems from a conflict between Pevsner and my pencil. Pevsner describes the tower as 'pretty west belle-cote, weatherboarded and painted white', but it is not a bell-cote as I understand bell-cotes. It looked to me like a small tower with a pyramid up on top.

I am thus presented with three alternatives. First to expand the spreading branches of the beeches on the left so as to obscure the tower beyond identification. That smacks of duplicity and the church has been involved in enough duplicity already. Second, to go back to Ashurst and do the sketch again. That's what my perfectionist wife would do — but not me, Third, tear the drawing out and forget Ashurst. That would be too much; I cannot bring myself to consign my efforts to the wastepaper basket. So I shall do nothing and let the confusion remain unresolved. Perhaps that is a fourth alternative.

The deceit in which the church was involved in the past concerned a supposedly miraculous relic which could be animated when the parson wanted to impress the gullible congregation. The device must have been persuasive, because, so it is reported, someone left it a legacy in 1524. I understand that fraudulent figures such as this were burnt at St. Paul's eventually, a ceremonial end which must, in a credulous age, have conferred some credibility on them as works of the devil.

There is a more respectable claim that Ashurst can press and this I saw by chance in the Kent and Sussex Courier on the day that I wrote these lines, 13th May 1983. Apparently, the first Wellingtonia seedling planted in this country was grown at Ashurst in 1850. Surely a more honest and satisfactory claim to fame than a gesticulating, mechanical contrivance.

LOWER HALSTOW
St. Margaret

Lower Halstow church is a dear little place. It stands at the head of a small creek which gives on to the wide seaward reaches of the Medway estuary. All around are mudflats and low marshy islets in one of which, incidentally, a lazaretto was maintained after the Great Plague of 1665 for quarantining possible victims of the plague. It is an appropriately isolated spot.

The church is old and originated in Saxon times. It is protected from rising tides and a sinking land by a sea wall which the monks who possessed the living in the middle ages constructed to safeguard themselves, their church and their 600 sheep. Most of the building now presents a 12th century appearance, although the walls, an irregular confusion of flint, ragstone and Roman tiles in herring-bone courses, imply an earlier church. In confirmation of my newly-learnt theories of structure, I was encouraged to notice that the nave walls, which support the substantial roof, are reinforced by buttresses, whereas the tower, with no great weight of steeple, is sheer. The impression of the compact little church within its ancient protective sea wall on the edge of the marshes is very nostalgic.

At the time I drew my sketch, my wife began an oil painting of the tidal creek immediately west of the tower. It was January and the wind blew freely across the estuary from the north — from the North Pole it felt like — and she found it a struggle to keep her easel upright let alone control her shaking paintbrush. I was more prudent and obtained some shelter from the sea wall and the willow. I also wore four jerseys which helped.

Until 1940, Halstow creek was used commercially by Thames barges, but no longer. Today, the creek is a haven for small boats of varying sizes and in various stages of disintegration. Untended craft lying at moorings or on the mud have a sad and neglected look at this time of the year. They do indicate prosperity though, perhaps out-of-town wealth from Chatham, or Gillingham, and one wonders how much of this affluence accrues to the church. We found it in good nick so I expect the nautical fraternity do not forget St. Margaret in their perils on the sea.

BOBBING
St. Bartholomew

Bobbing church stands against the road that links Sheppey to the main Dover to London route. So placed, it was once happily situated to offer spiritual comfort to the traveller on horse or foot. One might have expected there to be an inn in company to provide the complementary material comfort but there is no sign of one now. Today, the church is most unhappily stranded. With the transformation of Sheerness from a minor naval dockyard into a prosperous commercial port, the traffic has increased dramatically, and the road has become an unholy mess of construction make and mend. Eventually it will emerge as a smooth four lane highway and the traffic will thunder relentlessly past without a glance or indeed the opportunity to stop at the old church. Peace of a sort will have returned.

My new-found mathematical ego was flattered to find that Bobbing church also confirms the theory of the parallelogram of forces very nicely. With no cause for deflection of its downward weight from a vertical thrust, the west tower should have no need of buttresses. Nor are there any. But the walls of the nave, with the roof to contain, are properly well supplied with the essential props. So, here at Bobbing, where the church has been standing for 500 years, theory is confirmed by practice and result.

But wait, a disturbing thought occurs. The theory of the parallelogram of forces was first formulated in 1586, my paperback tells me. And the church was built in the 14th century, necessarily therefore without benefit of theory. Probably the masons of that unschooled day knew from experience how to keep a large structure upright but it is not immediately obvious to me that a tall edifice like a tower can derive stability solely through its own weight. One wonders if medieval practice would be confirmed by modern calculation. Does the diocesan architectural consultant ever, I ask, measure an old church like Bobbing and work out how the thrusts act on the walls? Perhaps he argues that the church is still standing and that a calculation is now otiose. No doubt such an expert opinion is correct, but I think that in future one should perhaps be a little circumspect as one scrutinises the plinths or stonework at the base of towers; certainly, one's fingers should be crossed in case the mathematics, like mine at school, is unreliable.

Internally, Bobbing is remarkable for a sedilia which arouses oohs and ahs amongst the cognoscenti who write the reference books. It was also the parish of Titus Oates who caused such a public stir in the anti-popery clamour of his day. He was an early example of a cleric who was not content to confine his pastoral work to his parish and one can think of a prominent cleric today repeating such extra-parish quasi-political activity. As the two profess different faiths, I wonder whether the latter would enjoy comparison with the former, but they do not seem dissimilar to me.

I was pleased with my sketch of the church at Wateringbury. It is one of those churches that do not permit a reasonable 'stand-off' view. Placed as it is on a slope above the Maidstone Road and surrounded on three sides by antique English yews, the untidy sort, there appeared no way in which one could do more than include an intimate fragment in the picture. Fortunately, the available fragment contained a distinguished monument and that, I concluded, made the composition. As a matter of fact, I have observed that the more competent artists favour a well-drawn close up rather than an 'over-all' picture. The really skilled seem to alternate between such a close-up and a distant view that simply suggests the church as the focus of the landscape. To attempt the latter, I would have had to invade the garden across the road belonging to a retired admiral and I did not think my artistic capabilities were up to that.

The monument that lends distinction to the approach to the church porch, as my drawing inadequately represents, consists of a cubed table tomb surmounted by five fluted urns. It is the property (if that is the right word) of the late Sir Oliver Style and the Latin inscription starts 'Felix lictor'. Having no Latin, I freely translated that as 'fortunate reader' which I found an encouraging opening. Oliver Style was the Crown's representative at Smyrna when that town was devastated by an earthquake in the 17th century and practically everyone but him was killed. He survived to be elegantly memorialised here by the Medway in 1702. 'Felix' certainly describes his fate; perhaps 'lictor' means consul and refers to him and not the reader of his epitaph. Pity.

Notwithstanding its appearance, Wateringbury is an Early English church. It is the tower in my sketch that conveys the Victorian impression and I was relieved to read in Pevsner that the shingled spire was rebuilt (redesigned?) in 1886, presumably part of the restoration mania that swept the country in the prosperous and confident reign of Victoria. We may now decry their efforts, but I dare say many churches would be in ruins today were it not for their well-meaning and thorough work of preservation.

Wateringbury church is the proud possessor of a 'dumb borsholder'. This is a rather unpleasant and primitive club, which, so they say, was wielded in Saxon times by a domineering tax collector to enforce his demands. It seems inappropriate for a church to give sanctuary to an implement of mammon unless it was tithes, not taxes, that were extracted from the reluctant locals. One can, in this case, imagine suitable threats of hell fire in the future accompanying menaces of immediate retribution from this truncheon to encourage anyone slow in meeting the just needs of the early church. Having recently completed my annual tax return, I am not sure that a borsholder might not be a preferable form of persuasion to the modern demanding return; one could perhaps dodge the former, or better, have one oneself.

BIDBOROUGH
St. Lawrence

Brita's mound or tumulus

This is a most attractive little church of Saxo-Norman origins. It stands commandingly on a spur of the Bidborough ridge which dominates the Medway valley to the north and the land that descends to the Ashdown Forest to the south. The church is made of sandstone, of some surprisingly substantial blocks; my reading of the geology of the Weald, which makes the ridge consist of 'Ashdown sand', explains the use of this material. It is perched at the limits of its spur and one can, with imagination, make out from my sketch the high retaining wall that supports the overhanging churchyard. The cottages to the east and west have something to look up to, and, if they occasionally get flooded from above, they may perhaps console themselves that it is a form of holy water. It all looks charming; the church pamphlet (actually a card with a drawing) presents the north aspect and very well it looks. My sketch, by concentrating on the lychgate, cobbled path and pollarded approach to the south porch, agreeable as these are, does less than justice to the church which I seem to have foreshortened somehow. One should always profit from any sketch available in the church; almost without exception, these display the best view and one is rarely a better judge than one's predecessors.

There are many tombstones standing in the churchyard and the one that catches the eye and rouses the imagination is that of a Countess of Darnley, buried in 1803. Bidborough seems a far cry from Scotland and Mary Queen of Scots. One does not expect there to have been such countrywide movement of the population before the advent of the railways or the motor car. Nowadays, residential life resembles musical chairs and movement seems continuous. The property advertisements in a local paper demonstrate this ceaseless fidget. I believe that the building societies maintain that the average stay of a family in one house is seven years. Which is better I don't know; to put down roots and rusticate, or to up-sticks, progress and belong nowhere. As a former naval officer I now prefer to be rooted rather than rootless. But what has this speculation to do with Bidborough church, you may ask; nothing, apart from the Darnley memorial and the way a stray train of thought can be aroused in a solitary churchyard.

48

OTFORD
St. Bartholomew

Otta's ford

Otford is the scene of battles long ago. First Offa, King of the Mercians, had occasion here in 774 to remind the men of Kent of his dominion in these parts. Then in the 10th century the Danes under Canute repeated the process. Arthur Mee records the fact, I am glad to say, that the Darent 'ran red with Danish blood' that day.

The church, as befits a battlefield church, keeps it head down. Its tower, built about 1100 is squat, square and keep-like; at its base the walls are four-and-a-half feet thick (no problems of sideways thrust escaping the walls here) and the abbreviated spire has the air of seeking to remain below the parapet. The wooden porch at the foot of the tower dates from 1637 and a testimonial to its carpenters it is. When I compare its condition after 300 years with that of the window frames in my own house, in spite of all the paint and my loving care, I begin to have doubts about our much vaunted progress.

Nearby are the remnants of the archiepiscopal palace built by Archbishop Warham, the property tycoon of his day. The palace suffered the usual fate and the unlucky Cranmer, who it is said worked on his prayer book here, was obliged to surrender it to Henry VIII after the latter's acquisitive march through Kent to the Field of the Cloth of Gold. Now the grandeur is gone and all that remains is a crumbling octagonal tower and fragments of a courtyard used as cottages.

For my excursion to Otford, I was accompanied by my wife, and dog, Boy. While I did the church, she began an oil painting of the typical Wealden house by the churchyard gate. This outing demonstrates another theory of mine, namely that women are more persistent and have more stamina than men. After an hour or so, I had finished my rough and, as Pevsner speaks respectfully of the interior of the pub, I felt justified in making an inspection. This I did with the dog, a smooth-haired fox terrier. To Boy's dismay, there was a fox-terrier fancier inside, and the dog's finer points and failings were dissected with a critical enthusiasm. All this took time but when we emerged my wife was still at work on the Wealden house and took a deal of prizing from her easel so that we could all return home for a belated lunch. If I hadn't been there, she would have foregone lunch and remained until the light faded or the paint ran out. I can never do that. However, notwithstanding my deficiencies, my drawing is complete and here in this book. My wife's painting is still unfinished; there must be a moral in this for the perfectionist.

PADDLESWORTH
No dedication

Paddlesworth is the oldest unaltered church I have drawn. It stands, surrounded by a farm on the fertile bed of gault that runs below the North Downs at the Medway gap and should not be confused with that other, similar Saxo-Norman Paddlesworth of East Kent near the Channel. The church, officially redundant now, consists of a simple chancel and larger nave and is Norman. If it were Saxon, it would have the distinctive pattern of long short stones at the corners of the walls. Rather like its companion church of Dode, a couple of miles away on top of the Downs, Paddlesworth was abandoned after the Black Death, the hamlet moved away (at any rate ceased to exist) and the little church was left to its fate. This amounted to total neglect, use as a farm barn several centuries later, and finally restoration to keep out wind and weather and formal categorisation as 'redundant'. A 1920s drawing of the church by Donald Maxwell shows the chancel with a lean-to on its north side and a brick chimney breast where the east window should be. There is also an open barn apparently attached to the west end. The whole effect is picturesque but derelict and only an expert would detect the tiny nave and smaller chancel from amongst the farmyard additions.

I don't suppose it ever possessed a consecrated churchyard; there are no grave-stones or churchyard cross which was what individual gravestones replaced from the 17th century onwards. On the other hand, since there was a church there once, there must have been people and, as we are mortal, there must have been burials somewhere about. If I were operating a plough or a mechanical ditch digger, I would keep my eyes peeled. In spite of its Norman provenance, Paddlesworth would well conceal a Saxon funerary treasure or, more likely, the relics of medieval peasantry.

It is rather a pity that that telegraph pole has to be quite so close to the east end of the empty chancel. Otherwise the little church looks perfectly happy amongst the busy and prosperous farm buildings. I would far rather lie where it is on the south slope of the Downs than amongst the unlovely civilisation of Snodland, its parent parish.

If I was the authority with responsibility for redundant churches in the diocese, I would plant a yew or two beside the church to keep it company for its second millenium.

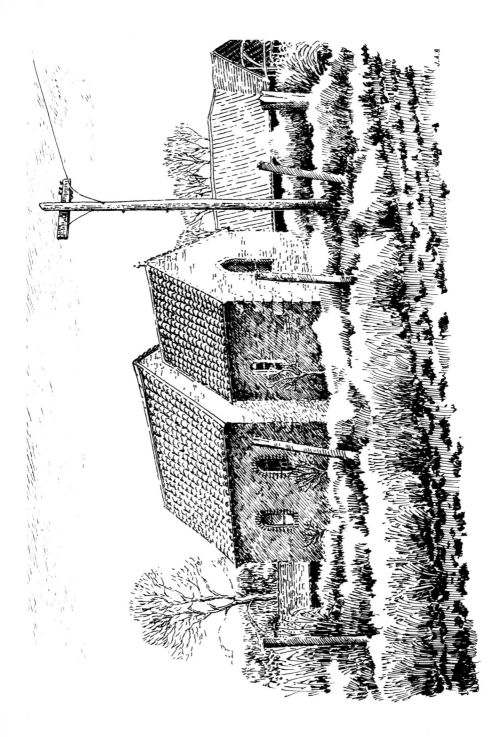

LAMBERHURST
St. Mary

Lambs wooded hill

The 14th century church at Lamberhurst has more the appearance of Sussex than of Kent. I think it is the recessed spire of shingles that gives this impression although the equal-length, isometric would be a more succinct term, chancel and south aisle are characteristic of Kent. Lamberhurst lies on the Kent-Sussex borders so the departure from pure Kentish tradition can be excused.

This once heavily wooded area was the centre of iron working in Tudor times, the wood being essential in the smelting and refining processes. Fortunately before all the trees were cut down it was discovered that coal did the job rather better and, to the lasting benefit of the Weald, heavy industry moved away to the north. The village was well known for its iron which was used in the manufacture of horse shoes, nails, cannons and cannon balls but its most famous usage was to provide the original iron railings around St. Paul's Cathedral.

It was raining sporadically when I made my rough sketch of the east end of the church. Raindrops do make the ink run maddeningly and I was frequently forced to suspend operations. Very annoying as Lamberhurst is one of those rare churches to offer a choice of view being open on three sides. One of these is the local golf course but I am glad to say the windows are out of range of even the most ill-directed golf balls. I particularly liked the large tree in my foreground, a chestnut I think it was, and the background of yews and pines against which the tower and spire show up quite well. I could have spent a lot more time at Lamberhurst.

As I left I was delighted to see a nuthatch. We used to see these handsome little birds at our last house at Wadhurst where we had a larch in the garden but here at Hadlow, amongst the orchards, nuthatches are absent and I hadn't seen one for years. Although I knew at once what sort of bird it was, I was unable to recall its name. This inability to enjoy instant recall of certain facts, in my case names, is I am sure a symptom of advancing years. I can still summon up mental images of things but not readily their proper or descriptive names. It seems as if the retrieval system of that part of my brain has deteriorated; if the image part of my recall system also evaporates, I shall be in something of a pickle. And that is why I am so anxious to write down these accounts of the weekly sketching expeditions that have given me so much pleasure over the past few years before they fade entirely from my consciousness.

BOUGHTON MONCHELSEA
St. Peter

Manor granted to Wain de Montchensie

This is the second of the Boughton churches that I have sketched but it is the first so far with a central tower. My reading of the reference works describes this type of church as 'turriform', representing the Byzantine style in England. That description sounds suitably romantic but the 'turriform' style belongs to the Anglo-Saxon period. Pevsner declares that this tower is supported by a genuine 14th century arch. Devoted as I am to the Gothic tradition, which spans the 14th century, I find the idea of Byzantium in medieval Kent more exotic and exciting; no doubt Pevsner is correct.

I had to make two descents on Boughton Monchelsea. On the first visit I attempted its famous lych-gate from an uncomfortable perch by the side of the road. By good fortune it came on to snow before I had had the misfortune to be hit by a car. On the second occasion caution prevailed and I reluctantly forsook the lych-gate; instead I was lucky enough to find the view depicted in the sketch. I don't know what it was doing there by a south-east corner of the church, but the writhing trunk of an ancient wisteria acting as a live canopy to a few select tomb-stones created an arresting effect. It is the sort of thing a far-sighted testator might demand in a will, together with the bequest of a small sum of money to the church-wardens to cover the annual care and maintenance of plant and its pergola. He would have to have been far-sighted (or a prototype of J.M. Keynes) to have bequeathed sufficient money to compensate for the ensuing inflation in modern times.

Like Ulcombe and East Sutton, its immediate neighbours, Boughton Monchelsea lies on the ridge that overlooks the low Weald. Hereabouts they quarried building stone over a period ranging from 1100 to 1850, or through the reigns of thirty three Kings and Queens of England — quite a span. Some of this stone went towards the building of Westminster Abbey. Without this contribution from Boughton Monchelsea and the preceeding parish in this account, Lamberhurst, the two major cathedrals in London would be the poorer.

Now, Boughton Monchelsea seems a far cry from the great works of London or the acts of Kings and Queens and much more suited to the thoughtless deer which graze peacefully in the park below the churchyard.

East Malling, not a big place, is an odd contrast of the past and the present. The church which is largely Perpendicular, built of the local ragstone and of the 14th century, stands at its centre and is surrounded by houses which are clearly past their first youth. And very attractive they mostly are. A family connection of ours bought a house here after his return from India about 1800 but I haven't discovered which one yet. East Malling must have been a very agreeable place to retire to in those days. Beyond the ageing houses that give the village its character is a belt of green fields constituting the orchards of the East Malling Research Station, two modern schools, now presumably combined into one comprehensive and the Victorian railway line which runs from Maidstone to London. And not far off is the threatening spread of Maidstone.

The church's battlemented west tower is imposing and presents its best aspect when viewed from the street leading directly towards it. To draw it thus would have meant placing my folding chair on the pavement or in the roadway and at the mercy of any passer-by. I did not feel up to that sort of scrutiny and so the full frontal was foregone. The south side with its equally battlemented stone porch and the east end with its large perpendicular window were both ruled out by the church-yard yews which effectively blanketed the target. Accordingly I settled for the unfrequented north side, as you see, with its orderly ranks of gravestones. I do like tombstones; they are so amenable to the pencil. Without too much loss of verisimilitude they can be moved as necessary to block a difficulty or open a vista. I can't remember whether I needed to move any of them in this sketch or not; I don't think so.

My visit to East Malling was the one occasion on which I have felt at odds with anyone in or around a church. On arrival here I found that the church doors were locked although inside an organ sounded. I rattled the handles but without result; there was nothing for it but to grind my teeth and get on with my sketch. Eventually when I was packing up, the musician emerged. He was returning the key to the vicarage, and if I wanted access to the church interior, I must in my turn draw it from the vicarage, he said. I made it clear, I hope, what I thought of such a selfish practice as locking the door behind one and, no doubt, I was thoroughly insufferable. At all events, the outburst relieved my feelings and may, on a future occasion, persuade the organ player to think twice before appropriating the public church for his own private enjoyment.

GOUDHURST
St. Mary

Goudhurst church stands on a commanding elevation (perhaps where the reputed Saxon battle may have been fought) at the head of the prosperous village street. The prosperity arose originally from the introduction of Flemings by Edward III in the mid-1300s to develop a national clothmaking industry. Then later in the 1700s the countryside became favoured by the gentry for their status-symbol mansions. All of which goes to explain the air of opulence and well-being that the church and village convey.

The west tower which we see beyond its arch of topiary yew dates from the mid-1600s, its predecessor having been destroyed by lightning and fire. Even my drawing cannot fail to make clear the classic design of the new west window, taken, so says the excellent church guide, from a design by Inigo Jones for a church in Leadenhall Street. But the rest of the church is much earlier and has 13th century origins. It is one of the principal sepulchres of the Culpepper family. Culpeppers, Culpepers or Colepepers are spread liberally throughout Kent and in this church their memorials range from 1400 to 1600. A seemingly excessive percentage of the wealth of the county must have been concentrated in their hands in their heyday. To judge by their effigies in some of the richer parish churches, no attempt was made by them to conceal or play down this accumulation of wealth and power; rather, the reverse must have been the intent.

Today, in a more egalitarian way, the wealthy are wise to adopt a less conspicuous display and where practicable to consign their fortune to some haven secure from the rapacious hands of the would be redistributors of wealth. Which is a pity. We, the general population, will not in future find for our delight the interior of our churches so richly decorated or interestingly filled with sculptured monuments to the great or worthy or wealthy. But maybe the envy of the levellers is assuaged by the imposition of swingeing taxation on the higher bands of income. There should be a balance in all this but wealth driven abroad by threats could otherwise be better spent on the permanent enrichment of our buildings. Preservation of our, with accent on the our, national heritage is the vogue phrase these days for such a point of view, and which envious taxation does nothing to help.

MOLASH
St. Peter

Molash is an extreme example of the remoter downland churches. It stands about half a mile from its so-called village — really only a straggle of houses and a pub along the Canterbury road — and has only a couple of period farmhouses to keep it company in the wide sweeping fields. Observing that there is no manor house present, one can't help wondering why the church is where it is but it has been at Molash from the 13th century nonetheless. What is more, it is not altogether insubstantial and must have consumed a disproportionate share of the locally available capital and labour in its construction.

The church door was locked, as one would expect, the key being available from the adjacent farmhouse. The farmhouse had a dog and the dog had a deep, menacing growl which discouraged overtures and which I found a sufficiently compelling argument against inspection of the church's interior. Pevsner does not have too much to say so I don't think I was deprived of any monumental masterpiece or architectural splendour. Behind me as I sketched was a paddock with a clutch of prize goats and they also seemed suspicious of a stranger. On the whole, the livestock of Molash were not after converts to the faith on the day I was there.

The outstanding external features of the church are its regular square tower, its red-roofed aisleless nave and the massive churchyard yews. My sketch undoubtedly makes a great deal of the tree in the foreground, which I remember as a yew, but have not convincingly represented as such. I have also made rather too much of the brambles; these do give one an opportunity to improvise as one will when one applies the final touches at home. The tower looks to me to be over-buttressed. Why they should be so substantial is not clear. Pevsner says that originally the tower was unbuttressed; how he can tell that, I also don't know but he probably had the advantage of an interior inspection. The upper courses, immediately below the parapet, are of brick construction so presumably something must have happened in the past to disturb the stone structure.

Another conundrum of the church concerns the screen between nave and chancel. It was transferred from the ruined and collapsed church at Eastwell. I can understand that a valuable screen should be removed for safety from a derelict building but why then install it in a church so obviously short of a congregation as Molash and far from the madding crowd so to speak. I dare say the diocesan authorities will have a suitable explanation and it is reassuring to know that they are careful to preserve and embellish their little-used and unpopulated churches where they can.

I have since learnt that the church is being restored and that it contains some valuable old stained glass; once again my uninformed speculations are confounded by the facts.

West Malling was one of the earliest parts of Kent to be settled by the Jutes; presumably these were 'Mealla's people'. They chose well and it is now a thriving little town of Georgian appearance. As such it should not really be on my list of village churches but being so near to Hadlow, I can hardly overlook it. It used to be known as Town Malling, I suppose to distinguish it from the much smaller adjacent backwater of East Malling.

There is a lot of medieval architecture to West Malling; not shown in my sketch but any description of town would be incomplete without the briefest mention of the Norman bishop of Rochester, Gundulf, who established the still extant nunnery in West Malling in 1100 and caused the forbidding keep, known as St. Leonard's Tower, to be built. The latter is supposed to be the earliest Norman keep existing in this country; very likely — it has a primitive look to it. A more recent claim to fame is the nearby ex-RAF airfield which rendered such distinguished service in the Battle of Britain; now alas it has become the offices of the Tonbridge and Malling District Council. Despite its present bureaucratic role, I am glad to record that the airfield buildings still retain their distinctive RAF appearance.

The church stands in a wide uncluttered churchyard with the town houses almost entirely concealed behind the church facade in my sketch. The west tower is early Norman with characteristic herring bone courses in its lower stages and supporting pilasters instead of buttresses at the north west and south west corners. One does not often encounter such features but they were early attempts at buttresses, I believe. The improved and succeeding version is the stepped variety, here shown at Malling in the south east corner of the tower. It is a very substantial tower and I would not have thought that the two pilasters contributed significantly to its stability.

Unlike the Norman tower, the conspicuous and elongated needle spire is of Victorian construction and, although from a distance it has a beckoning air, one wonders what possessed the Victorians to add such a prominent feature to a not inconspicuous and massive tower. They may have felt the church to be in competition with something somewhere — perhaps it was with the neighbouring Hadlow which received its 170 foot folly tower in 1840. If so, this church spire might also be classed as a folly.

SUNDRIDGE
Dedication unknown

Sundridge church stands, uneasily I would have said, on the north slope of the ridge that runs parallel to the very busy A25, Sevenoaks to Guildford road. It is fortunate to be well back and completely secluded from the roar and vibration and fumes of the ceaseless traffic which ruins the pleasant Kent and Surrey villages through which the A25 passes. But this is an early 13th century church and there can hardly have been a traffic problem then so why pick on a difficult north slope? Probably in those days of Chaucer, it was swampy at the foot of the ridge from effects of the young river Darent which flows through Sundridge and that may have been the reason for seeking the higher ground.

At all events, the far-sighted medieval builders set themselves a subtle problem by selecting a perceptible slope in preference to the river meadows. It must have necessitated considerable excavation to level the site for the church foundations; no doubt they had improved on antlers for digging implements by 1200 but I imagine that the picks and shovels of the day were not particularly efficient or plentiful for the work to be done. The church footings would have had to have been deeper and more elaborate than usual; some churches I have visited give the impression that they have simply been dropped on their site and are not secured in position by any positive anchorage to the ground underfoot. At Sundridge they could not afford to be so casual; the south walls would of necessity have had to be embedded deep in the ground with the north supported on some sort of levelling platform. These problems were compounded later by the addition of a south aisle to the backbone nave. Such musings concerning the difficulties of the slope would seem to be contradicted by that rough and ready buttress propping the south aisle. Instead of holding the church against the downhill pull of gravity, it appears to be compounding it. Quite the opposite of what one would expect. To be patronising, I would have thought the problem was beyond the skill of the 13th century but the church is still there where they put it 700 years ago. From the south side from which I drew it, it looks relatively snug; from downhill, the dark, sunless but well-buttressed north walls loom above one giving a gothic, precipice-like impression.

In more recent times the church has enjoyed the benefit of powerful families in the neighbourhood, always a cause, if not a guarantee, of good care and maintenance, not to say improvement, of the fabric. In the 18th century the 4th Duke of Argyll lived in Sundridge and his duchess is immortalised inside the church by her sculptress niece. Such a concentration of local wealth and power would undoubtedly have been to the advantage of the church. By all accounts some of it rubbed off on one of the rectors, the brother of William Wordsworth in fact, as both of his sons followed him into the church and were raised to be bishops in their turn. Another son of the village became a cardinal and one can perhaps now understand why the church would hardly have dared to slide downhill.

BRASTED
St. Martin

In contrast to Sundridge, its next door neighbour, Brasted church is set on the level ground, to the north of the dreaded A25 and well back from the village which was unwise enough to embrace the main road before the latter became a liability. From memory, I think the buildings shown beside the church include a public house and that is as it should be as churches and pubs go together in the country.

You would think that Brasted had avoided the problems of stability but something must have justified those enormous and numerous buttresses. They look very like afterthoughts, three to a face, and in the case of the central one on the west face, its builders had to make allowance for access to the west doorway. The result is that unusual hipped effect. Whatever the reason, probably subsidence, Brasted church can boast a very striking tower. I always like towers that are capped by a small, recessed, red-tiled spirelet; it seems a neater and more appropriate finial to a medieval battlemented tower than, say, a tall, slender spire like that at West Malling. The rest of the church is not so attractive as nave and transepts were rebuilt in 1860. I don't know why it should be but Victorian reconstruction, even when in character and impeccably executed, somehow fails to please. It may be the weather-beaten and time-worn look that gives the earlier stone work such a romantic atmosphere. Unkindly, Victorian church architecture puts one in mind of the Salvation Army — very worthy but not the sort of thing to stir the imagination.

And the imagination can be stirred at Brasted. Foundations of a Saxon church were found in the churchyard in 1966. Apparently it was once part of the territory of that king of Mercia, Offa, who caused trouble further down the river Darent at Otford. Replacement of the Saxon church began in the 13th century and replacement of the medieval church, as we have seen, was undertaken 600 years later by the conscientious, if extravagant, Victorians.

My sketch incorporates a lot of the churchyard. Prominent are those crosses in the foreground. I much prefer rectangular headstones, table tombs best of all, and I have unwittingly made my crosses too thin and skeletal. It produces a rather curious effect, almost as if the bones of the departed were pointing to heaven. Let us hope that that is where, in fact, they have all gone.

OFFHAM
St. Michael and All Angels

Offa's settlement

Offa again, what he was doing down here I can't imagine; the south of the Thames was the kingdom of Wessex not Mercia, but maybe in Saxon times Offa was a popular name like George is today.

At any rate, St. Michael's is a dear little unpretentious church consisting of a Norman nave and an equal-sized Early English chancel with an Early English tower clamped to the north side at the junction of nave and chancel. There was temporarily a south aisle, but after a hundred years, minds were changed and it was removed. Instead it was replaced in the 15th century by that robust stone porch which I have drawn. Since then, for the next 500 years, there have been no further structural alterations.

The church lies, looking towards the North Downs and well away from its village — presumably the Black Death at work again — surrounded on three sides by farm buildings. Indeed stone barns form the south limit of the churchyard and are no more than half a cricket pitch from the church door. I have always liked the atmosphere of this small church but regrettably it does not somehow lend itself to an overall view and I have, perforce, concentrated on the Plantagenet porch.

It all looked neat and tidy when I was there. Consequently I was not surprised when an elderly man emerged from inside carrying a bucket. With no-one else about he could hardly ignore me or I him. It transpired he was a volunteer and had been doing some amateur repairs to the internal plaster. After a bit he went off home and I went on with my rough. After a further interval, his wife appeared from the village. As chairman of the local Offham art society, she was naturally interested in anyone sketching her church and, perhaps scenting a new recruit she asked me back to tea. This pleasant encounter reminded me that, however unfrequented these country churches may seem, they all have their quorum of devoted and voluntary guardians. Living next to one at Hadlow, I am often embarassed by the fact that I make no physical contribution to its care and maintenance but only sketch others. However my wife helps with the flowers and that will have to suffice for one family until I finish this little book or paralysis attacks my drawing hand.

70

I never imagined that St. Mary, Kemsing would be as attractive as it turned out to be. The village of Kemsing itself lies on the cultivated plain of greensand known as Holmesdale running east/west between Sevenoaks and the North Downs. It can only have been a hamlet once but now is swollen by what, I would guess, are commuters to Sevenoaks and London. It does boast a well, named after the beatified daughter of a Saxon king and that may account for the quality of the ancient church. Its present state of preservation, though, must owe a lot to contemporary inhabitants.

While I was doing my sketch, the churchyard was invaded by the energetic children of a primary school under the care of their young female teacher. My spirits immediately collapsed but the party turned out to be unexpectedly agreeable and caused no disturbance so far as I was concerned. In due course they were given a brief talk on the interior by the vicar and I attached myself to his interested audience. The church interior is richly decorated and quite unlike some of the more austere, damp-ridden interiors one sees in country churches. The paintwork glowed and the carved woodwork gleamed and I could understand why the children had been brought here. The explanation, as always, was a rich and interested patron, in this case no lesser grandee than the late Governor of the Bank of England; in this worldly, irreligious age you can hardly do better than that. I suspect that he was more effective in material support than was St. Edith but she, of course, could have been the first cause in the establishment of the church and thus should take precedence over Sir Montagu Norman in any reckoning.

My view shows the west end with its friendly gathering of old tombs and its diminutive shingled bellcote and spirelet. Beneath the turret, the rough wall of flint and rubble was once rendered, but now, peeling and fading, its mottling produces a pleasant mellow texture. As it should observing that the church has Saxon origins. It has also, on the other hand, had more recent additions and I was surprised to read that the north aisle, seen here to the left of the bellcote, its west end looking correspondingly antique and weathered, was in fact put up in 1890. Apparently the north aisle window is a re-used Decorated one so I was not entirely misled by appearances. Another point to remember is that, although 1890 may seem like yesterday in terms of medieval churches, it does represent 100 years of weather — and there always seems to be a lot of that about.

COBHAM
St. Mary Magdalene

The village of Cobham has an extremely grand and individual church. It stands above the road that runs through the small period village and is surrounded on two sides by contemporary religious collegiate houses.

The church was virtually the private property of the Cobham family, built by them, as were the collegiate buildings, in the 13th and 14th centuries. Seeing that it was their creation, although they did need a Papal Bull before proceeding with the college, the Cobhams took care to make the chancel, where they proposed to be memorialised, larger than the nave which was, presumably, relegated for the less important use of their tenants.

And memorialised the Cobhams have certainly been. The chancel now exhibits the finest display of brasses in all England — so it was just as well when an enquiring antiquarian found them in an old chest in the church in the 18th century. There are nineteen brasses, spanning the years from the plantagenet Edward I to the establishment of the Tudor dynasty in 1500. They are dominated by an ornate and splendid tomb chest, date 1560, to the 9th Lord Cobham, his wife, ten sons and four daughters.

It is interesting to speculate on the relative positions of all these memorials. Doubtless the plum position is that nearest the altar and that has been appropriated by the 9th lord. The brasses, which have been thus upstaged, also generally support the proposition — first come, nearest the altar — and their dates become more recent as they are distanced from the sanctuary. They are all Cobhams, or husbands of female Cobhams, except that towards the end of the Middle Ages, four senior clerics from the college muscled in and joined the elite on the chancel floor. There must have been many other members of the Cobham family interred in the churchyard outside or in far off fields (one being killed on the Parliamentary side at the Civil War battle of Newbury) and one wonders how they felt then, or do now, at their failure to gain admittance to the coveted chancel floor.

Later lords of Cobham Hall, the Blighs, themselves not that distant genealogically from the Stuart kings, could only make it to the outside of the chancel walls where their monuments now stand. There is little doubt, therefore, that this handsome medieval church was intended to be, and in fact became, the Cobhams private chapel and their family passport to heaven and immortality. It has certainly succeeded in the latter objective and very probably in the former as well.

Lynsted is like a less well-endowed version of Cobham. The villages of both are now peaceful backwaters, both have enjoyed the support of landed families in the past and both contain memorials that excite the admiration of the pundits. In the case of Lynsted, two families, separately and individually, exert proprietorial rights over private chapels. In respect of historical personages, Lynsted lays claim to the daughter of Sir Thomas More; she married into the village, so to speak. Because of its outstanding display of brasses, Cobham must win in terms of numbers of those immortalised; from that of nobility of character of those associated, I think that Lynsted might have the edge. The church was locked when I drew it and I was unable to admire the famous monuments which so attract the attention of posterity.

Despite my disappointment, I was pleased with the outcome of my visit in the end. The church is not well placed for the artist being closely enclosed on three sides by yews and other evergreen trees and on the fourth by the village approach road which runs immediately below the three level gable ends of the chancel and chapels. These characteristic, equal-lengthed gables are what one would have liked to attempt but it would have meant sitting in the vergeless road or in the front garden of the facing tudor cottages. Not practical in either case and I, and any reader of these lines, are deprived of a rendering in this book of two Perpendicular east windows and a third of an earlier period. I expect that they would have been very difficult to draw accurately; these Early English windows with their flowing stone bar tracery are (I was almost going to say the very devil to draw — most inappropriate for an ecclesiastical window) beyond my capacity in the normal way. So there was really little alternative but to compress myself and my chair amongst the helpful headstones against the north side of the north chapel. The windows here are also Perpendicular but they do not dominate and are easier to reproduce. I was able, therefore, to focus on the interesting tower, flint in its lower half, weatherboard above and the whole topped off by a shingled pyramid spire.

It makes I hope a satisfying little sketch although totally failing to convey the importance of this village church or its general setting and architecture. In compensation, there is just a chance that those whom my headstones commemorate may not be displeased at this rare moment of attention. I would like to think so.

PLUCKLEY
St. Nicholas

Plucca's clearing

Pluckley is a small, close-knit hill-top village in mid-Kent — more a hamlet really. The 13th century church shares the perimeter of a tiny square with a pub, some period cottages and a village shop. There is, however, an identity to Pluckley and its neighbourhood, instantly recognisable by the idiosyncratic windows possessed by many of the habitations. These are the properties that once formed part of the Dering estate and legend has it that a Sir Edward Dering escaped from the Round-heads through one such window during the Civil War. Thereafter the Dering proper-ties were favoured by the installation of the distinctive windows with their semi-circular lintels. You see them all over the place in this part of Kent confirming that the Derings were great landlords for 900 years. Curiously enough, some friends of ours from America, when visiting this country last year, asked if we knew anything about Dering as the wife's middle and family name was Dering. Something to do with Kent was all she knew. If and when they come again, it will be a great pleasure to take them to Pluckley, the one-time headquarters of the Dering family.

When I drew the church, there was a stone mason working on the tower. An amiable man, he invited me up his scaffolding to inspect his work on the parapet. Naturally I wasn't going to trust myself to his ladders. In the sketch the tower looks somewhat modest but from the ground, it seems a long way up and, from the top, I know it would have seemed an eternity to the ground. And nothing on earth would persuade me to attempt that broached spire on top of the tower.

My drawing shows the footpath through the churchyard to the square. Obviously it is used as a village thoroughfare but nobody disturbed me as I sat on my chair. On the other hand when I had finished, I found the pub was packed which may explain the temporary absence or pre-occupation of the local inhabitants. They had better things to do than interrogate idle sightseers in their churchyard and, Pluckley being what it is, sightseers no doubt are a blight that comes in the summer — like the greenfly.

BIDDENDEN
All Saints

Biddenden has a glorious church, without a doubt, which looks particularly impressive when viewed from the village street facing west. It acts as a sort of full stop before the road curls decorously away and vanishes towards the countryside. Biddenden itself was a prosperous cloth making centre in the 1400s and today the old part, that is the street leading up to the church, retains its picture-postcard appearance. Of course there is the usual encircling ring of modern construction and that can't be helped. Without it, we shouldn't be here either, I suppose, so one should not make too much of a habit of criticising the 20th century.

What with additions, the church took 150 years to build in its entirety, completion coming around the year 1400. The architecturally discerning will observe that I have managed one Decorated and two Perpendicular windows; the latter style developed after 1400 so one can only conclude that these were subsequent changes to the fabric. Personally I am very attracted to those later Perpendicular windows with their flattened gothic arches which seem to have become the Tudor hallmark.

The church tower is noticeably prominent and sure of itself especially when seen from the west. Then, standing on its rising ground in the spacious churchyard, it commands the western entrance to the village and one can well imagine the authoritative effect it exerted on the medieval peasantry. Bend the knee, or else, it seems to say. I am always puzzled by the external stair turrets which are so common and which look as if they were just casually stuck on to the corner of the tower proper. That cannot in fact be so. One might have supposed that an internal staircase would have been incorporated in the original tower as a matter of established practice and such must be the arrangement in these towers not furnished with external turrets. This is what we have at Hadlow but here one only has to reach the first floor bell-ringing platforms. It is the tall parapetted towers which have the appendix turrets. Without them the towers would be plainer and quite often the stair-turrets are, in fact, emphasised by the addition of an ornamental weather vane on top. But they do seem to contradict that assumed maxim of nature which, roughly paraphrased, says 'nature never adds extra features or complicates systems where simpler ones will do equally well'. Ecclesiastical architecture invariably defies nature in this respect as also it confounds gravity with its soaring masonry.

KNOCKHOLT
St. Katherine

At the oak thicket

St. Katherine's, Knockholt, is in appearance one of the rare departures in country churches in Kent from the medieval style. It does, so Pevsner says, have two early Norman windows and these, I would suppose, are the two small, round-headed lancets that flank the triple lancet in the east end of the chancel. Otherwise the small church has an air of Mediterranean or Romanesque architecture. This comes, I feel, from the shallow pitched roof with its deep eaves. The simple flint tower, bricked at the quoins and placed midway along the south side of the church also contributes to an impression that is foreign to Kent.

Nevertheless, it is an attractive little church. The walls are rendered and this has faded and mellowed to produce a pleasant effect. The churchyard is surrounded by trees and the nearest visible habitation that I can remember is the ubiquitous pub — temptation consorting with salvation in solitude. It is hard to see how Knockholt church has managed to maintain its isolated situation. The village tends towards the north slope of the North Downs, the wrong and vulnerable side to the approaching tentacles of suburban London, and one can feel concern for the future preservation of its rural tranquility. There is luckily a Ministry of Defence establishment in the parish and that may be the source of Knockholt's defence against progress.

When I drew my sketch here, I was, for the first time in my peregrinations, disturbed by a funeral. I have also been unsettled by a wedding, as at Bredhurst, and even totally frustrated by one but, to date, I have not encountered a christening on a sketching expedition. I shall look forward to that event as being more encouraging than the Knockholt interruption and as a consequence of the Bredhurst type of ceremony.

Knockholt can make no great claim to historical fame. Arthur Mee remarks on a memorial to a V.C. earned in Palestine and to the fact that a summer house in which Dr Johnson sat at Streatham has been brought here. As my son is temporarily joining the Staff at Pembroke College, Oxford, of which Dr Johnson is the most illustrious graduate, I feel that one conscripted reader will learn something to his advantage — whether he will agree is another matter.

82

In my drawing, Hothfield church looks as if it might be in the heart of its village and facing the fenced-in green where cricket still is played. Not so; the church is nowhere near the village, being centred instead in what was once the Earl of Thanet's large park and this church, like many other country churches, lived in the shadow its great landowner.

I am uncertain of the age of the church; the nave was destroyed by lightning in 1598 but rebuilt immediately by its effective owner, Sir John Tufton, the father of the first Earl of Thanet. The tower is Deocrated but its buttresses are of 'rusticated ashlar'. My pen seems to have missed this subtlety but I have implied brickwork and this would suggest that the buttresses are post the main structure of the tower. Around the church are grouped the houses that were once part of the Thanet estate. The main house has been pulled down now and the glories departed. From where I sat, I had my back to an erstwhile walled garden — a sad waste as the garden bore no greater crop than weeds and long grass. I suppose that the estate had developed the dinosaur syndrome and been finally destroyed by the ruinous cost of today's labour. Nevertheless the combination of old church, converted houses, dovecots and abandoned walled garden, completely untainted by any hint of modern progress, produced a most peaceful and harmonious effect.

The church was locked. It is possibly redundant and the village may use a modern replacement nearer to hand. They would be the losers thereby. St. Margaret's is notable for its magnificent tomb of Sir John Tufton who rebuilt the nave after the lightning and entertained Queen Elizabeth — hence no doubt the Earldom for his eldest son. The tomb carries effigies of Sir John, his lady and their six sons and four daughters. All of this was dimly perceptible through the ancient windows and, as I peered, it occurred to me to speculate how many of those ten children, or indeed of preceeding and succeeding generations, enjoy comparable monuments. I think that these matters can only have been arranged on such a grand scale by the command of the occasional vain-glorious personage who wished to be so commemorated — a sort of personal self-service in stone. If it had been a regular practice whereby, say, all eldest sons in their turn received the honour, the churches would be momumentally overcrowded and there would be no room for the deserving congregation. As the younger son of a youngest son, I would have found this convention unattractive and objectionable.

EASTWELL
St. Mary

East spring

Eastwell church was a surprise. To judge from Arthur Mee's photograph, it was an orthodox medieval church standing by itself on the edge of a lake. The map marked no village; only an extravagantly large park which may have displaced any village that was the original raison d'etre for the church.

At all events, the church when I found it was as you see. Its collapse must have been recent but the remaining standing skeleton does not detract from the romance of the scene. In passing, one wonders idly what happened to all that fallen masonry. It was not lying where it fell or piled tidily to the side; it must have been thoughtfully carried away. Worked stone is always valuable, I suppose, and perhaps the church authorities use it economically in the upkeep of their still standing churches. Having acquired an odour of sanctity, I hope that this is so rather than in motorway construction.

The tower was Perpendicular and well-buttressed; the walls of the church were solid vide the deep embrasure of the shell of the window beside the tower. The chapel to the left, though, doesn't look right to me; it is as if it had been built after the collapse of the south aisle since it appears to intrude and that cannot be the case. A curiosity not explained or remarked on by Pevsner but I hardly think my observation can have been so mistaken as to imagine the intrusion. It does not matter now. If the chapel was originally built as a family sepulchre all the memorials have gone, the most elaborate to the Victoria and Albert Museum.

All that is save the most significant of all. This survivor consists of a few rough stones, in the form of a tomb chest that must have been let into the north wall of the chancel. Now the stones are overgrown with brambles and nettles and obscured by saplings. It is forlorn and does not at first attract the eye but, when it does, one can read the inscription on a small plate fixed to its side:

Reputed to be
The tomb of
Richard
Plantagent
22 December 1550

A forgotten reminder of the illegitimate son of Richard III, hidden down here before the Battle of Bosworth to escape the Tudor axe. He must have been young then but his life was long and, fortunately for him, inconspicuous for he survived his father by sixty five years.

WESTWELL
St. Mary

St. Mary, Westwell, must be the next of kin of the departed Eastwell. It is only a mile away amongst the cow parsley in deepest countryside but it is still there and in prime condition. Doubtless because its farming village and essential pub are there too.

The church is closely confined by the village houses and one cannot stand back to get a satisfactory overall composition. That's why I made do with a close-up of the south aisle, the 16th century porch and a glimpse of the steepled tower. The church as a whole is 13th century and possesses a most handsome interior to which I was denied access by the understandably locked door. 20th century vandalism has a lot to answer for. As sketches go, I was happy with this one; it was a first effort at the detailed representation of brickwork and seems to have worked, although the second, Decorated window could certainly be better. Incidentally, I can't believe that my buttresses are 13th century and, of course, neither can be the elegiac tombstones.

Unlike Eastwell, Westweel has led a tranquil existence down the centuries and no-one of note is interred there so far as I could tell. Therefore, when it came on to rain, I was able to leave without an uneasy feeling of stones unturned or inscriptions overlooked. Rain is one of the problems of sketching as it is of so many other outdoor activities. Writing, on the other hand, can snap its fingers at the weather. This wet spring of 1983, when all records for rainfall are being broken, is admirably designed for attempting these brief comments on my sketches of country churches. The endeavour is absorbing and enjoyable but in the normal way, if the sun was shining, I should be racked with guilt for neglecting the garden, the peeling paint on the windows of the house and the demands of the sketch book. I think, really, if one can write successfully, it must be a super career. All you need in way of capital equipment is paper and ink (perhaps a typewriter too) and these can be put to use in the most remote or idyllic spot you care to choose. The South Sea Islands (for R.L. Stevenson) or the Outer Hebrides (for George Orwell) were perfectly practicable but, in retirement, I find that Hadlow does pretty well for a beginner's purposes.

In this sketch, the tower of Bethersden church looks dramatically impressive silhouetted on the skyline of its churchyard. This is a considerable tower and it dominates the hamlet of off-right and below. One can well picture it as a beckoning signpost and I imagine that that is how the medieval villagers looked on it as they made their way home from the fields in the evenings. In the last war it was used as an observation post for sighting and reporting approaching German bombers; on the other hand it could have provided a sufficiently prominent landmark for them to have used it as a navigational aid in their run-in — a case of religion being a shade too impartial or neutral for comfort in time of war. To return to architecture, the tower was built between 1420 and 1430 and is made of Kentish ragstone reinforced by Bathstone; it is Perpendicular and well buttressed against the effects of weather and gravity and the parapets are prudently battlemented against the onslaughts of the enemy or the devil. Attended by its acolyte gravestones, there is now an air of premnaence and self-confidence to this typical Kent church.

Bethersden is known for its once sought-after 'marble' — a fossilised limestone quarried locally in the parish at a place called Tuesnoad. This ornamental stone was widely used for embellishing monuments and for accenting important parts of the fabric. So it was surprising to read that none is used in the construction of this tower although I believe that the tower at Biddenden, not far away, is made of it. The map reveals that the Tuesnoad source of the marble is, in fact, nearer to Smarden than to Bethersden and, geographically speaking, Smarden might claim to have been deprived of its geological fame. In a parochial way, Bethersden marble is reminiscent of the current Falkland Islands dispute but happily without such inconvenient consequences.

By pure coincidence on the day that I wrote these comments about Bethersden and its marble, the Greek Minister of Culture was here in this country to try and recover the famous sculptures from the Parthenon which we know as the Elgin marbles. I accept that there are counter arguments to her plea, or demand, but I must say that I think that she has right on her side. I should feel equally agrieved, although over a much less important article, if any of the treasures of these churches had been removed from their place of origin to fill a foreign museum. Fortunately for Kent, they have not achieved a comparably vulnerable eminence.

90

SNARGATE
St. Dunstan

Snare gate

Snargate church, on Romney Marsh, can make no great claim to fame, I think. It lies well back from the main road accompanied only by a house and a cottage. The omnipresent pub, rejecting such solitude, prefers to seek its custom from the traffic but where the church hopes to get its custom from is a mystery. It has an air of redundancy and perhaps there is none.

Its look of crumbling, mossy, disused almost, antiquity adds to its attraction. The tower is 15th century but the nave and aisles are earlier. How much longer the tower will survive seems to me to be uncertain. Beyond the tower, the ground slopes westwards down to the water-logged ditch that borders the small churchyard and the tower gives every impression of intending to make its way into the ditch. It definitely appeared to me to be out of true and leaning in that direction.

One wonders why such a relatively substantial church should have been built here on the Marsh. Sheep are the Marsh's most prolific crop and they do not, I suspect, require much in the way of human labour for their management; so where did the population to justify all these marshland churches — in particular the lesser ones like Snargate — come from? My two reference books contain only the briefest descriptions of the church and none of any village. The churchyard, naturally, has its quota of weathered tombstones but over a life of 600 years these would inevitably accumulate however few the congregation. I am sure that Snargate is today a headache for its bishop; of course he must hate to see it disintegrate and yet he cannot afford, or see valid reason to preserve it as the Victorians attempted in 1870.

My wife and dog came with me to Romney Marsh and Snargate. We had a picnic lunch and afterwards my wife began a small long-range watercolour of the church, the dog scratched happily around and I made my somewhat over-treed record of the church before it slides down into its watery dike. The sun shone and it was a perfect day lacking only one thing — a sight of an avocet which these marshes were supposed once to have contained.

92

OLD ROMNEY
St. Clement

Romney Marsh is full of old churches without much evidence of supporting villages and Old Romney, like the previously described Snargate, is no exception. It stands on a gentle mound surrounded on three sides by marshes on which sheep graze and on the fourth by a few old Georgian-type houses of warm red brickwork which contrast agreeably with the grey old stones of the church and churchyard.

My sketch from the west shows the square 14th century rubble tower nestling against its nave. I don't think it was normal medieval architectural practice for the tower to occupy a position against and in line with the west face of the nave. Such an arrangement rather isolates the tower from the body of the church but, at Old Romney, it has enabled a minstrels' gallery to be installed subsequently under that large decorated west window. This gallery, the box pews, a diminutive Norman arch to the chancel and accompanying squints, together all give the interior a cosy, old-fashioned and secretive atmosphere. Clearly there has never been any necessity to cater for a large congregation.

The tower has a broached steeple to support and for this it has two stepped, clasping buttresses that are carried almost to the parapet. No doubt the nave does duty for a buttress on the north side. There is no stair turret and, indeed, the whole church looks rather unlike the general run of Kent churches but then, I believe, that Romney Marsh has always held itself to be a place apart. Without external stairs to the tower one would expect to find some form of internal staircase. What the church has for a staircase proper is two tree trunks, sawn in half longitudinally, across which are secured the horizontal treads. This ladder looks serviceable, if distinctly primitive, and a surprise when one reflects on the skilful work needed to construct a broach steeple like the one here. It seems rather like spoiling the ship for a ha'porth of tar and is very idiosyncratic.

This old church, in its open churchyard, surrounded by marshes and sheep makes an arresting composition. We had another picnic here and both my wife and I have repeated this view in properly framed pictures; frames invariably help. It was summer when we were at Old Romney but I fancy that the church looks its best in mid-winter when the whitish tower stands out bravely against a wintry, snow-laden sky and the imagination is full of Dr. Syn and smuggling across the Marsh. I am sure we will visit it again.

Boughton Aluph is still a magnificent church representing, by its exotic, continental appearance, the pride of my collection. It stands on the slope of the North Downs overlooking the Great Stour valley and today, alone save for three or four largish houses, it has the aspect of the shell of an ancient guardian of the empty landscape. To describe it as a shell is grossly unfair to the well-wishers who raise funds and seek to restore and preserve it. And no doubt they will succeed for it is very well worth the effort.

The church is cruciform in shape with the 13th century tower and its associated stair turret at the junction of the nave, chancel and transepts. The walls are high and commanding and the mass of the building has the look of a fortress about it. Being built in the 13th and 14th centuries, when the opening salvoes, flights of arrows I should say, were first loosed to mark the start of the Hundred Years War, such an impression would not be inappropriate. And the church has been in the wars since then having been set on fire by incendiary bombs in the latest. The most recent attack, however, was that of the death watch beetle and only repelled in 1966. When I was there in September to draw my sketch, the porch doors were firmly locked and a printed notice announced that services were over for the year. So I had the churchyard to myself and the nibbling sheep. Sheep I don't mind, rather like in fact as they do keep the long, wet grass under control; it is barking dogs that are suspicious of strangers which I find disconcerting.

Later, on my first outing with the Friends of Kent Churches, I gained access to the inside of the church. The predominant impression is one of emptiness and space. The pews, apart from one specimen row, have all gone and the walls are largely bare, the hanging memorials having come down over the passage of time without replacement. With the Friends of Kent Churches on this occasion was an expert on old stained glass and we were given a learned description of the heraldic shields in some of the windows. These examples of medieval stained glass are small, faded as one might expect, and by now inconspicuous; but those whose coats of arms are here represented in glass were by no means insignificant in their day. The Black Prince, Edward I, John of Gaunt, Lionel of Clarence, de Vere, Mortimer, de Bohun and so on. It sounds like a roll call to the Wars of the Roses and that is the magical effect this church produces. Standing inside the nave, or outside in the solitary churchyard, one's imagination is transported from this material century to the romantic and violent days of the Middle Ages. And that is why Boughton Aluph takes pride of place in my collection of Kent country churches.

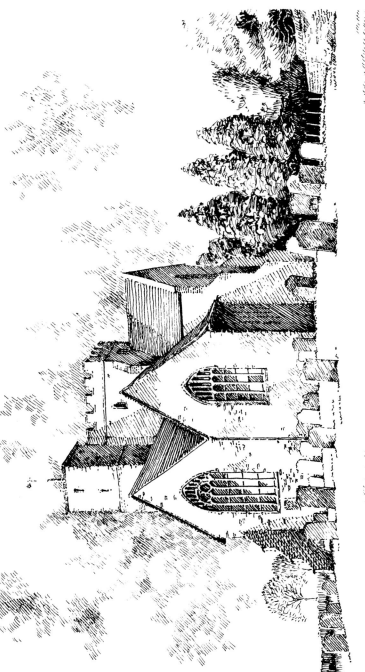

CLIFFE *Steep slope*
St. Helen

In terms of ecclesiastical hierarchy and history Cliffe must take a leading place, Councils of the Church being held here from 700 to 825, well before the coming of the Normans. As the village lies at the entrance to the Hoo peninsular which leads nowhere and is not on the road to anywhere, one wonders why it was selected for those Anglo-Saxon religious summits.

The church that I have drawn is the third to have been built on this site; the present version being almost entirely 13th and 14th century and I am glad to record that my excessive pre-occupation with stair turrets, or lack of them, was pacified by the construction in the 1880s of that circular projection shown climbing half way up the south side of the west tower. Cliffe has a very handsome church, described justifiably by Pevsner as 'a major parish church' and perhaps that is a consequence of its conciliar ancestry. One of the outstanding characteristics is the alternate banding of knapped flints and ragstone that decorate the walls of the aisles and transepts. I was, as well, impressed with the collapsing and self-important sarcophagus that occupies the centre of my churchyard — such elegant and time-worn aggrandisement can never give offence. Altogether the combination of church and well-furnished churchyard has a most distinguished appearance and that is surprising for those unaware of its origins when they contemplate the surrounding village. Sad to say, this is run down and pedestrian and looks quite incongruous beside the impressive church.

Immediately north of the church, the North Kent marshes stretch away bare to the Thames and this, of course explains the name as there is an abrupt drop from the churchyard wall to the marsh below. Standing there, with one's back to the church, one can see clear across the Thames to the modern oil refinery on Canvey Island with only the grazing cattle and estuarine birds in between.

The first time I saw Cliffe church and had my interest aroused was in 1941, when, as a sub-lieutenant in H.M.S. Quorn, a hunt class destroyer, which had been mined the night before off the East Coast, we were being towed slowly and gingerly past to be put to rights further up the Thames. That's over forty years ago and it gave me a particular pleasure to have survived those alarms and years to come back and make this sketch of a church which so attracted my early attention.

98

STALISFIELD
St. Mary

Stalisfield church was not easy to find. It hides itself in a network of narrow, unfrequented lanes on the Downs above Charing. There is no village and the general vicinity looks as if it has always been thinly populated. What the church is doing here to minister to one small farmhouse and a cottage is obscure; there is not even a great house near to justify its existence or to finance its building.

The church is 14th century, I suspect, modest in size, simple in construction and made of flint. There are few monuments of note although its rood screen does rate an honourable mention from Pevsner. It is precisely this type of small church, hidden in the Downs and attracting no attention from the sightseer, which will continue to mellow undisturbed and free of any trace of the commercialism now so prevalent and necessary where tourists abound. I find a forgotten church like Stalisfield preferable on my sketching forays to say Chilham, famous and grander and frequented as the latter may be. There was here, furthermore, a pleasant view of the church and its tower when seen through the bare and wintry branches of that large pollard in the foreground. Trees are difficult to draw convincingly but, like tombstones, they are helpful and there is never any difficulty when it comes to obscuring a window with tortuous and complicated stone tracery.

There was one disturbing incident to my visit to Stalisfield after I had eventually found it. As I circumnavigated the churchyard on my preliminary inspection I became uneasily aware of a sinister baying which sounded inappropriate to the surroundings. It turned out that next door, over the churchyard wall, there was a pack of bloodhounds in a seemingly inadequate pen. I promptly removed myself from that quarter and took refuge behind the pollard to draw my sketch. All went well with that occupation until I again found myself confronted with one of those bloodhounds. This time it was in the care of a young woman; she apparently bred them and was taking this one out for exercise. With their bloodshot eyes, I do not find this breed of animal endearing; why anyone should want to breed them as pets I cannot imagine unless they are intended as potential recruits for the police service. One can understand now what it may be that discourages the tourist from pestering Stalisfield. If that is so, every church should have its bloodhound.

THROWLEY
St. Michael and All Saints

Trough clearing

Like Stalisfield, Throwley has no village and its immediate companions are a few period cottages clustered around the solid oak lych-gate under which I sat to draw the church. It makes a fine sight with the path leading up beside the sentinel tombstones, past the gable ends of the nave and its escorting north and south chapels and so to the porch under the Early English tower. Seen from the lych-gate the church appears to crown the landscape and pierce the sky.

There is no false modesty to Throwley church for it has enjoyed the patronage of a succession of important landed families and both the side chapels reflect their one-time presence. The south chapel is the repository of a series of grand tomb chests to members of the Sondes family who became the earls of nearby Faversham in Stuart times. The north chapel contains monuments to the Harris family of later fame in the building of the Empire by the capture of Seringapatam in India and at the battle of Bunkers Hill in the revolutionary war and more recently still as president of the MCC. Obviously with such support no church is going to feel too straightened – whether it will continue to enjoy a similar good fortune in the future is another matter.

Throwley has been of consequence for centuries. One of my references quotes from the Domesday Monachorum of 1070 (which I take to be the inventory of properties attached to monasteries) that Throwley and Faversham each paid an Easter contribution to the Archbishop of Canterbury of 28 pence. Incidentally the humble Stalisfield, which paid 12 pence, was not so far behind. Consider their relative importance today – Stalisfield lost and forgotten, Throwley solitary and remote while Faversham has grown into one of the more prosperous towns of Kent. The reason must be that ribbon of development, the A2 Dover to London main road, which is the source of Faversham's wealth and population and why the other two hamlets have declined into obscurity on the sidelines.

In its youth, about the year 1150, the patronage of Throwley was granted to the Benedictine abbey at St. Omer in Northern France. It is not clear what advantage was obtained for Throwley from this early example of 'twinning' any more than is it obvious what benefit is gained by our towns today which so ostentatiously announce their 'twinned' continental siblings. In both cases the arrangement seems more beneficial to those in authority than to those who pay the tithes and taxes.

TEYNHAM
St. Mary

Teynham church, fortunately for its peaceful seclusion, has been deserted by its modern and unlovely village which now stands astride the A2, a mile or so away. Teynham is thus comfortably preserved in its past amongst the orchards and on the edge of the Swale marshes. Not far off, the Swale penetrates the marsh to form the small inlet of Conyers Quay; twenty years ago we had a picnic there and the quay was little more than a silted mooring for derelict Thames barges and to quote Arthur Mee 'it is like walking backwards in time to reach it'. Now, a generation on, Conyers Quay is a crowded yacht repair basin with an increased resident population. It surprised me to see what a change could come over somewhere in the relatively short space of twenty years and this during the country's so-called economic collapse. Teynham being a backwater, it may not yet have heard of this fashionable complaint.

I suppose that Teynham is mainly noteworthy for Henry III's Tudor gardener who introduced cherries into England in this parish. That achievement is a legacy which any man would be glad to leave behind and any parish to claim. Otherwise Teynham has been singularly tranquil down the years although I don't doubt that the invading Jutes, Saxons, Danes, Romans and Normans all passed this way en route to the spoils of this island.

The church is Early English at the east end and Perpendicular at the west end. Its square tower is conventional with regulation buttresses and battlemented parapet, but no stair turret. What one doesn't see so often is the dormer window in the roof and the two, small clasping lean-tos on either side of the west front of the tower.

When I was at Teynham there was snow in the air and it was bitterly cold. The roof and tower were under repair and the two young workmen owned to being perished. While I had my back to a tombstone for shelter from the wind, they brewed tea inside the bottom of the tower to recover from exposure at the top. I could well imagine that the wind up there cut like a knife and a January on the open marshes of the Swale estuary seemed hardly the best season for such work. Very probably they will restore their frozen tissues with a Spanish fortnight beside the Mediterranean later in the year.

This little white church at Fawkham has a thoroughly unassuming air of well-cared for simplicity and austerity. It is in fact something of a rarity, a genuine Norman church that has remained virtually unaltered since its original construction. In plan it consists of a small rectangular chancel attached to a somewhat larger rectangular nave, the latter crowned by a miniature octagonal wooden bellcote. There are no buttresses, no side chapels or aisles and no transepts. It does, however, make minor concessions to softer generations by the provision in the 14th century of a south porch and the enlargement of some of the narrow Norman windows. The whole uncomplicated structure puts one in mind of the long-abandoned Paddlesworth except that Fawkham is still in use, for weddings especially I was told, and very much looked after.

I remember I saw it on a Sunday morning about noon well after the service and the congregation had departed for their lunch. Inside, one of the local ladies was still clearing up and she was only too ready to discuss the layout and the faded, near-indecypherable wall paintings, especially the one that had recently come to light, literally and figuratively, in the splay of a tiny window undergoing replastering. The nave was clean and uncluttered, somehow having escaped the accumulations of ages. Outside the unenclosed churchyard seemed to merge into the surrounding meadows with only the scattered tombstones to distinguish between the two. It all looked so neat and trim and when I said as much to a man exercising his dog, my remark was very well received as it transpired that he was the volunteer who cared for the churchyard.

I hope that my sketch conveys the idea of this ancient Norman church amongst the sweeping folds of the Downs. It lies in a valley that leads to nowhere in particular and with little modern development to change the character of the landscape and none to modify the church. It is in fact a well-preserved antique, rather like a precious piece of antique furniture but, since it is immovable and firmly anchored to the ground, it has stayed where it is in deepest Kent and avoided export across the Atlantic or exposure in a museum's glass case. So much the better for us.

This picture of St. Mildred's at Nurstead represents one of the few instances when I could achieve a satisfactory stand-off view and I enjoyed putting, in the foreground, the barn with its rusting corrugated iron roof, the rickety gate opening onto the empty field and the gaunt hedgerow trees. It looks as if it could come on to snow and it was a winter's day. Nurstead church is lucky to remain unencumbered by civilization; in fact the limit of the overgrown village of Meopham is only half a mile away. One would never think so and Nurstead must be one of the few churches to benefit from the presence of British Rail which acts as an iron curtain to halt the northward spread of Meopham's houses.

As medieval churches go, Nurstead is straightforward with its reassuring Perpendicular tower. There was a church here at the time of the Domesday Book when the rapacious Odo had the manor. Later, in the days of King John, the lord of the manor paid his feudal dues to the crown by performing twice yearly 'ward duties' at Dover Castle. That may not sound such an imposition as most people's mortgage payments today but it must have been quite an expedition to travel from one end of the county to the other without the help of British Rail or British Leyland. The lord of the manor probably lived in the adjacent Nurstead Court, now the relic of a great medieval house. Today it is of such historical architectural interest that it receives forty one lines from Pevsner compared to the meagre ten he gives to the church. It is not often that a village church is so upstaged. Incidentally there is no village here, only the court which looks to be heavily into farming.

Writing these brief, amateur comments on my medieval country churches has made me realize what an odd frame of mind one develops with advancing years. I now find that it is only the old that attracts and it is the modern which repels. If one's mind acted logically, this surely would not be so and I dare say it would not have been a characteristic of the Victorians. Why then should it be the hallmark of the late 20th century when the luxuries of life are so abundant? I don't think it is only me who has such a biased outlook; societies like the Friends of Kent Churches would not exist if it was. Very likely if the symptoms persist and I survive another decade, I shall have retrogressed further and become an Anglo-Saxon enthusiast. Not so much of their manifestations is left to wonder at, though, and what can be found is rather more inscrutable, I imagine.

Otham church stands far too close to Maidstone for its comfort and before long the tentacles of housing that have spread along the A274 and the A20 will capture this scattered and defenceless hamlet. The village in fact, is more noteworthy than the church through possessing, as it does, a collection of outstanding timber-framed houses. One feels mildly envious of their owners until one remembers the servant problem; these houses are not small or labour-saving and they were designed to accommodate large families with their retinue of domestic staff. Who can afford either these days and the future of country houses of distinction leads in the direction of the museum rather than the family.

The church is somewhat disparaged by both Pevsner and Arthur Mee for being so restored that its time-worn medieval charm has been obliterated. That may be so but I think it looks very handsome in my drawing. The receding ranks of lichen-mottled tombstones in the foreground convey a realistic two-dimensional effect; the difficult perspective of the gable end and of the gothic window arches is roughly right and there is no sign of Maidstone so I find Otham, pace Pevsner, attractive and one of my more successful efforts.

I like the tower with its weather-boarded belfry stage. I admire the broached steeple but I am always puzzled by these. They look complicated and contrived and one wonders why a more straightforward pyramid cap was not adopted or why a steeple was required at all. I have never seen inside a broached spire but I imagine that their construction was along the following lines. First, the skeleton of an octagonal spire was erected within the rectangular top of the tower. That would leave a small triangle exposed at each corner of the parapet. In some cases these hidden triangles were roofed with lead; in others the builders were more ambitious and constructed four sloping surfaces to meet the octagonal spire a quarter of the way up. This was the broach and the junction of the four angled planes with the eight planes of the octagon produced those four gussets of inverted triangles which are so hard to draw respectably. The whole structure would then be tiled and there you have your spire with its contrived pinched effect. There remains the question of what supports the octagonal framework within the tower and for the answer to that I believe we are indebted to the squinch arch from B.C. Persia. It is a nice, but probably mistaken, thought that some of the architectural character of this country derives from Alexander the Great's murderous march across the plains of Iran to the banks of the Indus. Doubtless some will find this theory extravagant and ridiculous; it appeals to me, nevertheless, and I could not bring myself to exclude it from my text.

HIGHAM
St. Mary

It was shortly after Christmas when I decided to add the inconspicuous Higham to my collection of churches and I thought I had persuaded my daughter to accompany me to this fringe of the North Kent marshes but no, a tactical cold intervened and she was thus deprived of an introduction to the nostalgic pleasures of ancient, romantic and unfrequented churches. Perhaps she will get around to these when she reaches my age. She has, however, since more than made up for her January lapse by painstakingly deciphering and typing a great deal of my manuscript. I am accordingly much in her debt.

Higham was remodelled in the 14th century but despite its isolation at the end of a very, very minor road, almost a track, it has a history of early importance. Iron-age coins have been found buried here and, behind me where I sat, farm buildings overlie the foundations of a Benedictine nunnery. This was established by the Norman king, Stephen, in 1150 and there is a canopied tomb in the church to one of its abbesses.

I liked the unpretentious appearance of the venerable church, hugging the ground against the blast, and made of ragstone banded with knapped flints to give it its distinctive striped effect. Apart from the farm, there is a straggle of cottages inland but one feels that with the departure of the nuns, I suppose at the dissolution of the monasteries, and the arrival of our secular age, the justification for such an isolated church has vanished. It is surprising that it is not redundant.

The churchyard walls are crumbling and the gravestones look lonely and derelict but, in fact, while I was sketching a family arrived to tend one. As it happens the churchyard now has literary immortality; Higham disputes with Cooling, also on the edge of the marsh, for the honour of being the original of Dickens' scene in 'Great Expectations' when the escaped prisoner from the hulks moored in the Thames was surprised by Dickens' Pip. I believe Higham the more likely spot but either church would be appropriate. I have never much cared for Dickens, I know one should, but he is heavy going to me and I prefer Jorrocks to Pickwick. Nevertheless his imagination has probably served to prolong the life of both these romantic but redundant churches whose raison d'etre has long since departed.

WEST KINGSDOWN
St. Edmund

King's Hill

The church at West Kingsdown has had a lucky escape. It lies a mile back from the A20 which at West Kingsdown is a depressing ribbon of bungalows, cafes, garages and passing cars. This road has a lot to answer for but here it met its match in a rector who was determined to preserve his Saxon church. Somehow he raised the money to buy the surrounding woodland and now the church hides unseen behind its curtain of trees and undetected by the world at large; it is as if the church has taken refuge and the trees are its bodyguard.

The nave and its south tower are Saxo-Norman, the chancel being slightly more recent. Compared to the broached spires we have discussed earlier, the simple pyramid cap on the tower looks appropriate and effective. On the other hand, the low, squat buttresses look ineffective for their purpose of providing stability to the tower. It is, of course, entirely presumptuous of anyone to criticise the construction of a church tower when that has remained upright for a millenium — one should remember that. I shall be very gratified if the brick garden wall which I built remains upright for more than a few years.

My sketch, I hope, does manage to suggest an ancient church enclosed in its woods and left to its own devices. Unexpectedly though, it was open and within, a flower lady was topping up vases. She was proud of her church, communicative and distinctly put out when we could find no guides. I gathered that the vicar could expect to hear from her. Later, while I sat sketching in front of that imposing tomb in the foreground, an old man approached and offered his copy of the guide. He and his very arthritic wife lived in a wooden bungalow amongst the trees, the only habitation in sight. When I eventually returned the guide, his invalid wife examined my rough sketch with the eye of a connoisseur; on the walls of the bungalow were her by no means incompetent efforts from the days before her bones seized up.

I enjoyed my encounter with this church and its custodians. I am sure the rector who saved it would have approved of the three people I met that day I was there.

JAS

CHILHAM
St. Mary

Cilla's settlement

Chilham village and church stand on an eminence which overlooks the Great Stour where it breaks through a gap on the North Downs on its way to Canterbury and the Channel. The site has long been settled, I suppose because of its military potential, and there are prehistoric graves nearby and the ruins of a Roman, Saxon, Norman castle. The church, however, is 13th and 14th century and very fine. Like its neighbour Throwley, it was twinned with the Benedictine abbey at St. Omer but this arrangement, I am glad to say, was suppressed after a bare 100 years or so in 1400.

In my sketch we are looking up the path that leads to the battlemented, stone south porch and the Perpendicular west tower. It is winter and the distinctive chequer pattern of flint and Caen stone can be made out through the bare branches of the intervening trees. It was also perishingly cold. I was surprised to read that the octagonal clock face on the tower is 200 years old — no built-in obsolescence there obviously. Later I revisited the church with the Friends of Kent Churches and could examine the interior, for which this church is noted, under expert guidance. One enters through the foot of the tower, not through the elaborate south porch, and finds oneself in a rich nave which clearly has long enjoyed the patronage of the locally prominent. There is some medieval stained glass, said to represent the Popes of the day, which Cromwell's destructive Puritans missed; there are some large, grey tombstone flags, ledger stones I believe they are called, which make such an austerely appropriate floor for any church, and then there are the monuments. I cannot forbear to remark on that to the wife of a lord of the manor. She is commemorated by an outsize column and associated allegorical figures which entirely fill the little south chapel. The combined memorial is wholly inappropriate to the space available and one only hopes that the lady's accomplishments in life were commensurate with her monument. As she appears to be unknown historically this seems over optimistic and there must be many members of her family, and indeed the parish, who as a consequence cannot find room in the church and must await their salvation from the churchyard outside — which incidentally is no bad place to be.

It is sad that such a beautiful spot as Chilham, with its period village square dominated at the north end by the medieval church and at the opposite south end by the imposing gateway to the 17th century mansion, should be so atmospherically spoilt today. It is the motor car and the tourists with their leisure and liking for things past which are the trouble and any enjoyment one may derive from admiring the church in its setting is dissipated by all the others doing the same thing. I expect that this last paragraph could be described as a thoroughly selfish comment. As indeed it is.

BADDLESMERE
St. Leonard

Badlesmere church is deserted by its village, if it ever had one. It stands lonely on the North Downs above Charing with its only companions a farm house and farm buildings. To my mind, Badlesmere is infinitely preferable to and more attractive than a well endowed church at the heart of its busy village like, say, Chilham. It is fortunate that the North Downs are well supplied with these remote little churches so much to my taste. As I was drawing, a car drove up and out popped the driver. She was, she said, the lady churchwarden and lived in the farmhouse by the churchyard wall and my pleasure in drawing her church appeared to be equalled by her pleasure at finding that someone should want to do so.

As you can see from the drawing, the church is simple to a degree; an Early English chancel and nave, a plain little tower with its wooden bell chamber perched on top and that odd little battlemented south porch; the rendered walls peeling and fading; yet with nothing much to write home about, the church in its churchyard somehow manages to make much more of a picture than say, some of the better-known village churches with their more sophisticated and ambitious architecture. I am not certain why this should be so and, no doubt, there are many who would not agree with me. Inside it is equally unpretentious and fortunately unimproved by the Victorians. By chance the box pews were overlooked and remain to remind one of a Georgian congregation listening to some interminable and, dare I suggest, dogmatic sermon.

The church also contains a carved bench end illustrating diagrammatically the Holy Trinity and providing thereby the clearest explanation of this theological mystery that I have yet seen. I won't attempt to describe it though.

Badlesmere is about five miles from Boughton Aluph; one of the medieval stained glass shields at the latter is attributed to 'Badlesmere the Rebel'. There was a Badlesmere beheaded for denying Leeds Castle to his queen and perhaps it was he. In that case he would have been better advised to have confined his activities to his delectable church at Badlesmere.

LEAVELAND
St. Lawrence

Leofa's land

Leaveland church is a short half mile to the west of Badlesmere and it was the lady churchwarden of the latter who pointed it out. They share the vicar, as do many of these minor parish churches, and one must wonder, as I do, why the Plantagenet landowners or church authorities found it necessary to erect two small churches so close together. I find it difficult to believe that there can ever have been a sufficiently numerous population to justify the duplication but perhaps there were tithes to be extracted. That must be a possibility.

Leaveland church is, if anything, on a smaller and simpler scale than Badlesmere. The nave and chancel are Early English, a small bellcote takes the place of a tower and the unbuttressed walls are mainly flint with the occasional Roman tile which, I suppose, the masons found lying around the site and economically pressed into service. The open churchyard is fairly well furnished with tombstones, some elaborate like that to the right of the path and, in general, Leaveland is better stocked in this respect than Badlesmere. The disparity may be due to the presence of a large 16th century black and white house, Leaveland Court, next to the church and which outranks Badlesmere's prosperous farm house.

Both churches thus have their one accompanying habitation but are otherwise solitary. One cannot help reflecting as one wanders round the churchyard or examines the crumbling, roughened masonry, what may have occurred down the years while the church has been standing in this downland countryside. It was all settled so early in our history by the invading tribes from North West Europe, the people of Leofa, no doubt, followed in turn by the acquisitive church under the see of Canterbury and finally by the farming community. Once the land must have been available to and held by those who lived off it; the coming of the Normans with their feudal society put paid to that primitive form of land tenure and now, in the 20th century, although we may own our houses, we are essentially a landless society. The land is still there, as beautiful as ever, but it is in the hands of a microscopic proportion of the population. Maybe that is why the countryside is dotted so liberally with churches; they seem to belong to all of us and one can feel, in their churchyards, that one has as much right to stand and stare in these lonely places as anyone.

Hartlip reminds one very much of Lynsted. Both are set in small villages on the north slope of the Downs in the strip of fertile land between the A2 and the M2. Hartlip is the more vulnerable being situated between Rainham and Sittingbourne, neither neighbours one would select for choice. Both churchyards overlook the village street at their eastern extremities and both churches terminate in a triple gable of chancel and north and south chapels. There is unfortunately insufficient room for a sketch from this direction before the sunken road intervenes and, unlike the churchgoers, we are denied this typical Kent signature.

Seen from the west, Hartlip church appears to consist of a strong Perpendicular tower with no half measures about its south west stair turret and a wide reach of red-tiled roof stretching away to the east. It was extensively restored in the 1850s and much of the rustic decay made good by the conscientious Victorians to the visual disadvantage of the church. I think that it is the renewal of the pointing that so effectively spoils the patina of the old stonework; I suppose it is necessary and without it, I dare say, the damp would be more prevalent and destructive than it is. The restoration appears to have been particularly thorough at Hartlip. For some reason the original west doorway at the foot of the tower was found wanting and replaced. Happily a strange conceit persuaded the authorities to re-establish the discarded arch of the doorway in the churchyard wall where you see it in my sketch. I was, in fact, sitting in an adjacent hopfield. This hopfield, the usual serried ranks of carefully organised hop poles and steel wire rigging, slopes away towards Rainham in the distance; there was no well-trodden footpath that I could see nor any of those useful and ubiquitous signs for the ramblers so who could be expected to enter the churchyard from this direction — not the seasonal hop-pickers for sure.

In its present position, the ancient arch seems to serve no useful purpose but at least it has been preserved to stimulate the imagination, rather as Stonehenge does in its far grander scale. Not many country churches can boast a medieval arch in the least frequented corner of their boundary wall and Hartlip, I think, has scored a small point thereby.

Cooling church, like Higham, stands on the edge of the North Kent marshes in the empty Hoo peninsula. All around are the market gardens and fields that supply London and, with little in the way of population, the church has been declared redundant. The season in which to view and draw it is winter when the trees that ring the churchyard perimeter are bare and leafless and one can then admire unimpeded the tall tower silhouetted against the wide sweep of the distant Thames and the level countryside.

It is a 14th century church built of ragstone and consisting of chancel, nave and west tower, the latter supported by its substantial, diagonal flint patterned buttresses. Like Higham, Cooling claims to be the site of the Dickens' scene in Great Expectations when the escaped convict is startled by Pip. Be that as it may, there exist certainly the thirteen bodystones of the children of two local families which so excited Dickens' compassion. Inside the church, at the west end of the nave, are three rows of 13th century benches, the prototypes of our conventional pews. They are much smaller than the seats of today, because medieval physiques were less robust, I imagine, and they convey an extraordinary air of antiquity. I wonder that Dickens did not incorporate these evocative old benches in his novel as well. I don't know why but those three rows of worn old benches seemed a perfect illustration of the vast gulf which separates the rough and primitive life of the Middle Ages when all these churches were built and the greatly enlarged and enriched lives we enjoy today.

Cooling had a surprise for me — its castle. I knew nothing about this when I first came to Cooling and was astonished on rounding a bend in the road to find myself passing the ruins of a fortress hidden low in the marshy ground. Subsequent investigation revealed that it had been built in 1381 by a Lord Cobham after the French had sailed up the Thames in Richard II's reign. The defiant gateway still stands undefeated by time and is now in the proud ownership of the Wardens of Rochester Bridge. Worthy though they may be, the Wardens hardly sound as romantic as the umpteenth Lord of Cobham.

When I learnt my naval history at Dartmouth in the 1930s we rarely lost a battle at sea. It is disconcerting later in life to find the French sailing up the Thames with impunity, to learn of them sacking Winchelsea on a dull afternoon when they could find nothing better to do and, the final indignity, to read about their manoeuvres with hostile intent off Spithead in front of Henry VIII and his unseaworthy flagship. Evidently it was considered prudent to edit history before its submission to young and impressionable minds.

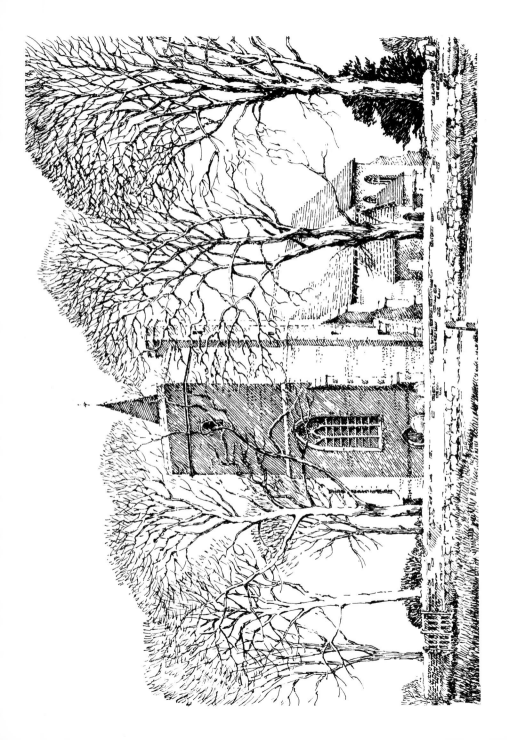

LUDDESDOWN
St. Botolph

Luddesdown is not easy to find amongst the winding valleys of the North Downs above the Medway where it develops from a river into an estuary. It is not a populous place; there is no adjacent village, just one house and a Victorian village school. The house, which stands close beyond the churchyard wall is the more remarkable and pre-dates the church, having iron age origins followed by Saxon, Norman and Tudor ingredients in its make-up. I would have liked to make a closer examination but these solitary country houses tend these days to be infested with dangerous and truculent dogs to discourage the loiterer who could have criminal intent.

The church is not large; 13th century and much restored so that it too has a Victorian look to it, dark from the overcrowding trees and not given to sunlight. Wandering round the churchyard I was reminded very strongly of M.R. James' marvellous 'Ghost Stories of an Antiquary' Luddesdown is exactly that sort of place and one half expected to catch, out of the corner of one's eye, the fleeting movement of something rather disturbing as it scuttled from behind a collapsed headstone; or to find oneself being hypnotised by the compelling runic script, barely discernable, on an ivy-covered memorial. I regret that my drawing does not manage to catch the haunted atmosphere of this isolated church in its cordon of yews and evergreens; I was driven to seek out a view from the edge of the churchyard where the trees had not yet put out their leaves and the spring sunlight was allowed to penetrate.

Strangely enough I was not exactly alone. A young female student artist appeared also to sketch the church. I expect that I put her off, or I may have resembled one of M.R. James' less attractive creatures, for she withdrew to attempt the Victorian school — who its pupils might be I could not imagine. It happens that this particular area of the Downs is wanted by the Army for manoeuvres or something and she had been commissioned to make a few sketches before the past becomes obliterated and the magic dispelled by high explosive. I was glad that I too had had the good fortune to anticipate those forbidding notices — 'War Department — Keep Out'.

St. Gregory and St. Martin

In spite of its undoubted air of grandeur, Wye church presents a puzzling aspect. From where I sat to make my sketch, facing the tower, one would normally have expected to be looking at the west end. This is not so and, here at Wye, the tower is unconventionally at the east end of the church. What apparently happened was this. In 1686 the original Early English tower fell down carrying with it the chancel and transepts. The tower was conscientiously rebuilt in its former style but the eastward range of the chancel and transepts were left unrestored; instead the chancel was abruptly terminated level with the tower by that semi-circular apse. As a restoration policy, such economy does seem to me to demonstrate a mistaken set of values. I have always understood that the chancel, which contains the altar, represents the most sacred part of the church and that the tower is a less-essential addition serving principally to emphasize the rest. Why then concentrate on the inessential at the expense of the vital?

At all events, the restoration has left us with a very fine tower, complete with finials at the corners of the parapet for added stability — no doubt a lesson learnt from the previous experience. It was a misjudgement I feel, however, to install the clock face so clumsily that it obscures the belfry apertures. In fact as a general rule, I find clock faces on medieval towers anachronistic and out of place. They are no longer needed by the parishioners and they often fail to tell the time; away with them, I say, and let the tower stand with its architectural purity undefiled by modern mechanism.

Wye, beside the Great Stour above Canterbury, has always been important to the Church and, in the 15th century, the then Archbishop had a college for training priests built against the churchyard walls. It still stands today and has successively since been a grammar school for boys and the agricultural faculty of London University which it now is. It is diverting to speculate which role is the more necessary; the training of farmers perhaps, for without their efforts we none of us would be here; or the school for boys, for without them there would be no future; or the college for priests, for without them, they would maintain, there is no certainty of the hereafter. My money goes on the farmers, without the present there can be no future and without either there can be no hereafter. But without a belief in the hereafter there would be no churches to admire or draw. So?

BRABOURNE
St. Mary

Broad stream

I came to Brabourne by mistake and very glad I am. I never enjoy driving along motorways and, on this occasion, when heading for the more famous church at Brook, I found myself locked on to the M20 which my out-of-date map failed to show now reaches almost to Folkestone and it was only a few miles inland before I could escape and retrace my way by country lanes. First Stowting showed up but I by-passed its 'restored out of existence' 13th century church and then I was unexpectedly rewarded by the treat of Brabourne.

This hamlet stands in a fold under the Downs with its church at a bend in the road amongst a coherent group of red-bricked 18th century houses. These all matched in period and quality and must, I suppose, have been estate houses once. Although I doubt if the papers or mail are ever delivered before noon, one could be very comfortable and cosy in Brabourne, I would think, particularly if one had farming or botanical interests. The world of motorways and fast travel seemed to be light years away.

The church, which is late Norman, may look over ambitious for its few parishioners but it does make a splendid composition to paint or draw. The tower is outstandingly solid and durable-looking although appearances may belie reality because there has been near catastrophe in the past. It is evident that the south west corner at one time began to disintegrate and here the flint and rubble masonry has been replaced by worked stone reinforced by three of the most massive buttresses I have ever seen used to prop up an unstable tower. The name of the village may provide an explanation — broad stream. This brook runs from the Downs above, along the churchyard wall, and could possibly have flooded periodically causing the foundations of the tower to crumble and subside.

It is as well that this church continues to stand for it contains a small Norman lancet window said to be the oldest complete window in England (who checks the validity of such sweeping claims, I wonder). Not being an aficionado of stained glass I was unaware of and failed to notice this national treasure and, not for the first time, kicked myself for failing to look up my references beforehand. As I am frequently and tediously reminding my wife, no-one can be blamed for making a mistake the first time but only when it is repeated and that is precisely what I did at Brabourne. The inflexible motorway that led me there must be my excuse.

Brook church was something of a disappointment for me. From the photographs I had seen I expected to find a lonely and windswept church, deserted apart from a few sheep and the rooks wheeling overhead. This was not the case at all. Instead I found a church, certainly very ancient, but set conspicuously on a mound beside the road that knits together the strands of Brook village. Conscious of the importance of their church, the village look after it and all is neat and tidy with the grass cut and the church gleaming like a polished antique. One almost looks for a sign saying 'This way to our famous church'. Clearly it is lovingly preserved but, sadly, for me its medieval atmosphere has been manicured away.

And Brook is undeniably famous and ancient. It was built in the first few years after the Norman Conquest and displays a unique sequence of 13th century wall paintings — some fifty faded medallions set around the walls. Externally, however, it is the square, austere and unbuttressed tower that dominates. This is remarkable for its relative size and for the vestigial, rectangular, stepped stair turret. I have never seen one quite like Brook's version; it puts one in mind of a Babylonian ziggurat and one wonders who its builder was and what happened to him. Perhaps he had been on a Crusade and was influenced by Middle Eastern architecture. The effect is so original that the builder must have left his signature elsewhere; no doubt Pevsner would know.

Contemplating the church before sketching, I was forcibly impressed by the overwhelming importance claimed by the tower in the make-up of the building despite the far greater significance of the chancel and nave in terms of function. The disproportion seems incongruous. If I were asked to design a building to provide a small, sacred chancel, a larger space for the congregation and facilities for bells, I should place the emphasis in that order with the bell apparatus a poor third. The chancel would have a slender spire pointing to heaven to proclaim its purpose, the nave would be attached but unostentatiously and the bell tower separate — probably at the entrance to the churchyard. The path to the church porch from the detached bell tower would be lined with tombstones to remind the churchgoers of their mortality and all their contributions would be collected in the porch to free the area of worship of any taint of earthly materialism.

No doubt it is just as well I did not adopt architecture for a career but if I had wanted to design churches for a living, I was born at least 600 years too late. Few are built in this secular age.

GODMERSHAM
St. Lawrence

Godmaer's settlement

Godmersham church occupies an enviable position above the River Stour which flows past the foot of the churchyard. Behind the church, on the slope of the Downs, rise the woods and parkland of Godmersham Park; facing the church the wide Stour valley, crossed by an ancient Roman road, now the A28, brings the sound of the 20th century to intrude on the rural tranquillity. Godmersham is a tiny capsule of the past.

The church is an odd combination of Norman construction and Victorian restoration. Why the Victorians should have wanted to restore so conscientiously a church that serves no more than a great house, its estate cottages and a farm is a mystery for the congregation must always have been limited. Externally the north side is unrestored Norman and the more interesting part; this is the view that my wife and I each sketched from deep in the nettles and set about with forgotten tombstones. The tower is the original, unbuttressed Norman and is supported at its foot by an unusual apsidal chapel, facing us in the drawing. This chapel can only be reached from inside the tower and, as all its doors, both internal and external, are either long-locked or blocked, I don't suppose anyone has seen the inside of this remarkable feature for a long time; I doubt if the bells have been rung for a long time either. Built on the slope above the Stour, there must have been settlement problems and that could be the reason for the energetic Victorian rescue operation. Their work is manifested by the two massive brick buttresses at the corners of the chancel; clearly these are effective as witnessed by the unbroken squares of tell-tale glass let into the fabric of the walls. Inside the church is rather gaunt and empty with damp the pervading impression.

There has been some publicity for Godmersham lately and that may explain the roughly scythed churchyard grass and the few flowers in the church. After the death of its owner, Godmersham Park was recently sold for an astronomical price, followed by an auction of its contents for an equally astronomical sum. Godmersham Park has been one of the great houses of Kent for over 200 years and yet there is no evidence in the church, or elsewhere that I have read, that its many owners have been prominent in the history of this country by their deeds or by the offices they held. Despite their inherited position, their lives were unremarkable and are unrecorded except for one individual and he by proxy so to speak. He is memorialised in the church but we only know of him because he was Jane Austin's brother. It is a salutary thought that generations of squires left no impact on this church to compare with the occasional visits of a Hampshire parson's daughter.

RUCKINGE
St. Mary Magdalene

Rough meadow

Ruckinge comes as something of a shock as one drives along the road which marks the inland boundary of Romney Marsh. The village itself is unremarkable but, on rounding a bend in an easterly direction, one is suddenly confronted, point-blank, with a massive and venerable church tower. It seems to defy one to drive past but the traffic behind more insistently defies one to stop. It is the traffic which thus saves the church from over-popularity and preserves its air of undisturbed antiquity.

My sketch was made from a meadow just outside the churchyard to the south. Behind me ran the Royal Military canal and beyond stretched the Marsh to the sea. I would have preferred to attempt a closer view of the Norman tower in order to suggest the ancient crumbling stones and the primitive belfry windows, apertures would be a more appropriate word, but the difficulties of the immediate local surroundings and the claims of composition denied me. I can't remember a church with such a weathered appearance and one hopes fervently that the restorers can be prevented from getting their hands on it. It looks a perfect monument to a vanished age as it is and restoration will almost certainly destroy its time-worn look. The church is of Norman origin, Saxon they said in the pub, and possesses two fine Norman doorways with the characteristic zigzag moulding — one of these, now blocked up, can be seen in my sketch.

Inside the church is plain and rather bare; not even Arthur Mee could make much of its interior, perhaps because there are no memorials. It is the first church in my experience that exhibits no memorials whatsoever to anyone other than the list of vicars. They said in the pub that this was because no-one of any wealth or consequence had ever lived at Ruckinge. Somebody must have once or there would be no church; it is a curious absence. In actual fact, the only parishioners to qualify for note are two smuggler brothers who were hanged for robbery in 1800 and whose remains are commemorated in the churchyard by a rough uninscribed plank supported horizontally by iron stanchions. For a church that is solid and substantial to have produced no more than two smugglers to celebrate in close on a thousand years is surely unique or unreasonable. It has such a splendid old tower and such carefully moulded Norman doorways that I cannot believe that Ruckinge has always been inconsequential. If it has left no recorded mark in history, it is thoroughly romantic now and must lift the spirits of all who travel the winding road from Tenterden to Hythe.

136

Kenardington church, although unlocked when I was there, seemed to have the air of a redundant church. The nave was, indeed, furnished with rows of chairs but it did not look as if it had held a congregation for some time. That may be an injustice but my impression is corroborated by the church's approach path which runs through the carefully mown lawns of the one-time vicarage. For the occupants of the Glebe House, as it is now entitled, it must be rather like having a private church of one's own without the responsibility for its upkeep; an enchanting and singular conversation piece to have at the end of one's garden.

Apart from its unusual approach, Kenardington is an interesting church which has clearly seen better days. There is more than one blocked window displaying evidence of delicate tracery, a circular stair turret to the Early English tower and the base of a small shaft mysteriously embedded in the east face of the chancel wall. In its youth the church boasted both a nave and a south aisle. The nave went after a fire in 1599 and the aisle was economically substituted to replace it. Signs of the disaster can be seen in the bricked up tower arch and the traces of the roof abutment to the tower. The permanent replacement north wall with its four supporting buttresses which was given to the south aisle (now nave) suggests that the decline of Kenardington must have been accepted locally immediately after the destruction of the original nave. In its present remote situation, surrounded on three sides by open fields, that decision indicates an accurate early appreciation of its likely future status.

To my mind, the most interesting feature was some faint scratched marks, vertically scored, on the jamb of the porch's inner door. These enigmatic marks are not mentioned by either Arthur Mee or Pevsner but they did not seem modern, I thought. They were, as best I can reproduce them, as follows:—

What such cabbalistic designs can mean, I cannot imagine but I am sure that M.R. James would have enjoyed interpreting them.*

The air of mystery which pervaded this church was reinforced for me, when wandering round the empty churchyard, I disturbed a sleepy little owl which startled me as much as I him. On a mid-summer afternoon the atmosphere was calm and unclouded; alone in the autumn twilight, it might be different. I would like to think so.

* I have since learnt that these scratches are stonemasons' monograms. Presumably it took eight of them to build this church.

St. Mary the Virgin must be one of the more remote churches in the county. It lies hidden on the north slope of an isolated valley on the crest of the Downs above Wye. There is a farmhouse and farm buildings below the church but otherwise nothing apart from the cultivated fields and the traces of the vanished forest. The village itself is out of sight above the valley and there seems no conceivable reason why church and village should be so separate; it must have told against a good congregation and collection when attendance meant a good half an hour's walk along an unmade-up lane there and back.

The church is extraordinarily attractive in its simplicity and antiquity. It is very old; 13th century tower with an earlier nave and chancel. It is largely made of flint reinforced at the corners by worked stone. There are buttresses here and there of a later date than the walls but at the east end of the chancel is a pair of those prototype buttresses, pilasters, which are of Norman design and one sees so rarely. They are so rudimentary that they cannot have been too effective and, not surprisingly, were invariably replaced by more solid constructions. Inside the church, which I was delighted to find unlocked (too remote for vandalism?), there is evidence of blocked up Norman arches and one minute Norman window. Internally this window has a deep wide splay but externally its dimensions are roughly eighteen inches by six inches. It is on the north side and that may explain its mini aperture. There is a small organ, said by the guide book to come from Cobham Hall — the other side of the county — and this instrument betrays its grand provenance by the quality of its top class mahogany which one doesn't normally see in church organs. The church also retains undamaged its 15th century rood screen and exhibits traces of undecipherable wall paintings. Apart from the deal pews which unhappily were installed as replacements for the original oak box pews, the church is unrestored inside and out. It is a marvellous relic of the past and an enchanting place in which to spend a solitary autumnal afternoon with sketch pad and pencil. Long may it remain unfrequented in its valley on the Downs.

Despite the two hours there and a determination to overlook nothing, it was only when miles away at home that I realised that I ought to have examined those worked quoin stones to practise my amateur dating. One of my paper-backs on parish churches explains knowledgeably that one can roughly date worked stones by the bolster marks on them. At Hastingleigh the quoin stones looked much more recent than the flint walls they edged and a little beginners' detection could have confirmed or contradicted this surmise. Life is full of missed opportunities; this occasion was a minor irritant at one's short-comings and at one's tendency to think of the right thing to do only when the opportunity has slipped by.

PEMBURY, Old Church
St. Peter

Stronghold of the Pepingas'

This was the third and most successful (artistically) of my visits to St. Peter's. It lies, isolated by woods, some distance from the growing dormitory village of Pembury, and was only recently saved from being declared redundant. This fate would have been a pity for the church is ancient and interesting and deserves to survive for another century or two of animation.

Its original part, the ironstone nave, dates from late Norman times and is clearly distinguishable from the 14th century additions of enlarged nave and tower commissioned by John Colpeper. It is said that he used his wife's money to finance the construction and certainly he recorded his debt to her by having her family coat of arms displayed in stone on one of the buttresses to his new chancel wall. Nor did he neglect to commemorate his own on the adjoining buttress. This extrovert behaviour was subsequently copied by another prominent family, the Woodgates, whose estate in the 18th century included 'the perpetual advowson of the vicarage of Pembury'. So now the buttresses, north and south of the chancel, are decorated by small stone shields bearing the arms of one-time local grandees. It is curious how often such families, seemingly impregnable in their hey-day, have vanished from the scene; despite generations of wealth and privilege, there are no Colepepers or Woodgates to assert their presence in Pembury now.

The church is kept in apple-pie order and credit for this must go to the verger who was also responsible for my enjoyment on this occasion. He happened to be present, conscientiously superintending volunteer 'flower ladies' and, being naturally talkative and devoted to his church, he was only too ready to enlighten me in great detail about the fabric, the history and the finer points of the church. He also looks after the replacement Victorian church in the centre of the village and, having been a printer, he edits and illustrates the joint parish magazine. Here is a man who has undoubtedly found a most agreeable and rewarding occupation for his retirement.

Externally the crowded churchyard contains one very unusual table tomb — that shown against the south wall by the two Colepeper buttresses. According to the verger the occupant had a morbid fear of being buried alive. Consequently her coffin was lidless and, in return for her estate, her butler was charged with providing a meal every day for a year. There was a grill at the end of the tomb for the purpose and apparently the curious could thereby inspect the bones of the entombed lady. It is an odd story and all the more bizarre when one reads on the inscription that she was only thirty four at the time of her death in 1803, long before the unreasoning fears of old age could have unbalanced her mind. The grill is now removed and the aperture bricked up. One presumes that the butler faithfully completed his part of the bargain; history or the verger does not relate what happened to him but he would have had disappointed relatives, as well as a vengeful ghost, to contend with if he failed in his charge. Not a risk that I would care to take.

142

St. Peter's church is famous for its monuments to past inhabitants of the ancient village of Ightham. Those in the sanctuary are particularly ornate and grandiose and extol virtues and achievements that one would not dare to question. Such vainglory may be good for reputations but yet seems inappropriate in a church whose teachings glorify the humble; nevertheless we should be the poorer without such arresting and historic memorials to past generations. The stone effigy to the recumbent Sir Thomas Cawne, a contemporary of the Black Prince, has not, however, enjoyed the respect the knight might have expected. He lies, in full armour, very wasp-waisted, and some iconoclast has had the temerity to carve his (or her) initials on his leg. It is difficult to understand why anyone should want to commit such a vandalism.

As in practically every church, there is a list of vicars, reaching back as far as history can trace. Here at Ightham, they also record the patrons of the living and it is interesting to read that the first of these is baldly stated as 'the King'. Stupidly I failed to note the date but it must have been twelve something, the king a Plantagenet and he probably held land here at Ightham.

From my viewpoint, the church presented an attractive appearance, especially the south porch with its differing shades of rubble sandstone. Within, the splendid oak door pre-dates the Armada by thirty years. Like all these old church doors, it is double skinned, rather as the hulls of yachts used to be, and was clearly designed to keep intruders at bay when necessary. Happily it was unlocked when I was there.

According to the church guide, the tower is original and dates from the late 14th and early 15th century. The masons must have economised on the stonework as all its corners and buttresses have had to be reconstructed in brick. The north aisle was also rebuilt of brick in the time of Charles I and presumably that was when the west tower was reinforced. Since that date, for some 300 years, the church has successfully withstood, unchanged, the ravages of time. But it has not suffered from neglect to judge from appearances. While I sketched, the grass was being cut (October) and the interior polished. Considering its age, its embellishments and its charming village, this attention is no less than St. Peter's deserves.

The rural village of Birling, below the Pilgrim's Way under the North Downs, gives every appearance of an estate village, as no doubt it once was, and appropriately the church provides corroborating evidence of the patronage of generations of the Nevill family. The village street runs between the one-time tied cottages, past the pub to the practising smithy when a sudden bend takes one under and around the high retaining wall of the west end of the churchyard. Perched on top, a few feet from the edge, the 15th century Perpendicular tower looks down dangerously and a circumnavigation of the church takes one perilously close to the ten foot drop to the road below. One hopes that the footings of the tower are well consolidated by now. The oldest part of the church, in fact, dates from the 13th century and is the south wall of the nave; those narrow windows shown on either side of the church door are representative of the period.

Notwithstanding its impressive appearance and position, this simple church is more interesting inside than out and this, not surprisingly, follows from the presence of past members of the Nevill family. They are commemorated by several shields (twenty I should say, not having counted), displaying the coats of arms of 17th and 18th century Nevills, which decorate the chancel walls. One can imagine Warwick, the Kingmaker's approval but also his opinion that Birling might be a trifle inconspicuous and unfrequented for the relics of such an historic family.

One of the Nevills, the 4th Earl of Abergavenny, was vicar of Birling in the 1850s and his three daughters are credited with the carving of a tall, intricate, gothic, Victorian, wooden font cover. The church pamphlet says so; Pevsner more cautiously says 'by several ladies' but I find it difficult to believe. The font cover is so unfeminine and one cannot envisage aristocratic ladies, probably technically inexperienced, indulging in such exacting and fiddling cabinet making. Although Birling is remote and little more than a hamlet — population 460 — there must have been more exciting things for the ladies to do. However they have the attribution and thereby a memorial to ensure their continued remembrance.

I always browse around the churchyard on my sketching outings as much as I inspect the interior. The atmosphere of the past is more vividly conveyed by the ancient yews and the collapsing, time-worn tombstones. Birling exhibits a relatively conventional collection of these, nothing remarkable, but here I was rewarded by a yucca in flower. I have never seen one of these exotic shrubs in flower before and it did present a somewhat singular appearance amongst the damp long grass of the churchyard. But then, equally so, twenty heraldic shields and two tilting helmets are hardly what one would expect to find, as a normal thing, in the chancel of what is now a very minor church.

I had been looking forward to the church at Graveney; it gets high marks from Pevsner for the quality of its interior furnishings and for its unreconstructed 14th and 15th century external fabric. I was also expecting perhaps too much from its geographical setting on the edge of the Swale marshes, west of Whitstable. In the event the church was locked and I missed my chance to admire the rood screen, still in place, the sedilia, the piscina, the brasses and so on.

I therefore had to content myself with a churchyard exploration. As Pevsner says, the church is a rarity for being so 'delightfully unrestored' so that one can still enjoy the mellow grey walls of flint and rubble stone. My sketch attempts to suggest the effect these differing weathered materials make; it is wholly satisfying to the eye. One hesitates to contradict so eminent an authority as Pevsner but I did happen to find a flat coffin stone immediately west of that west door commemorating a Victorian incumbent and crediting him with responsibility for the restoration of the church and its bells. Perhaps, in this instance, the work was carried out more sympathetically than is usually the case. At all events, were it not for this tombstone and the south porch, Pevsner would be reliably supported by appearances.

The solid south porch looked, to my inexpert eye, to be contemporary with the rest of the church but unfortunately it must have been in the reverend gentleman's time when they stuccoed it. Happily, time and weather have worked their benevolent magic and the effect is not too disastrous. The porch was unusual in my experience in that it contained no notice of any kind whatsoever. No indication where the key might be found, no lists of flower arrangers, no edicts from the bishop, no church accounts, no anything. From the welcome of the porch, one could imagine that the church is redundant but I don't thinks this to be so.

Standing on raised ground above one of the many streams that flow north into the Swale channel, one might have expected the church to be surrounded by an attractive village. Perhaps it once was, but not now. Its immediate neighbour is the conventional, substantial farmhouse and farm buildings; a few 1920 farm cottages keep it company at a respectful distance but otherwise the vicinity seems to exemplify the depopulation of the rural countryside. Farm workers are no longer needed in quantity when tractors and combines of various sorts are available and this consequence of modernisation has obviously reached the North Kent coast. Possibly that explains the somewhat forlorn air of this handsome medieval church. Not that that detracted in any way from my enjoyment in sketching Graveney church in the autumn solitude; probably my pleasure was enhanced because I now remember it with solicitude.

148

'Blink' they said in the pub, 'and you will pass it.' Too clever by half, I thought, but they were right nonetheless. Pass it I did and I was glad to be able to retrace my way unobserved. The church lies some 400 yards back from the road, next to a prosperous farmstead (a latterday Godwine?), and it is reached along a narrow causeway between potato fields and paddocks. Clearly a motorised congregation has never been expected as there was nowhere to park or even turn; just a small overgrown churchyard acting as a full stop to the causeway.

The church is diminutive, early Norman and devoid of buttresses, and puts one very much in mind of Paddlesworth, that abandoned and redundant chapel under the Downs above Snodland. Here the church consists of a small rectangular nave, with west bellcote, attached to an even smaller chancel. There are four minute Norman windows and a vestigial stair turret leading to a long departed rood loft; the stairway must have been designed for dwarfs for it gave me claustrophobia merely to contemplate it.

The only relatively recent feature is the early 19th century north porch. This depressing construction was a mass of cobwebs, bird droppings and nesting material and gave every appearance of neglect. Fixed to its wall was a notice, dated March 1983, proposing that the church be declared redundant. For this proposal to take effect, said the notice, an 'Order of Her Majesty in Council' is required. It seems rather like using a sledge hammer to crack a very small nut. Anyway the church door was unlocked so presumably the Council had not met by the time of my exploration, October 1983.

Inside, the disorder of the porch was repeated. The effect conveyed to me was that of a dinner table not properly cleared away. I don't know with whom responsibility for such matters as tidiness rests but certainly one rarely sees the vicar doing the church chores. Whether it was my responsibility or not, if I was the vicar, I would make it my business to spend an hour or so clearing up the inside of Goodnestone church. In general, I suspect that the sight of the parson wielding a scythe or operating a lawn mower in the churchyard would do more to attract a congregation than any amount of diocesan committee work. These old churches are so marvellous and irreplaceable that I find it extraordinary that their vicars don't spend more of their time there; to my way of thinking, one could not find a more appropriate or rewarding place in which to demonstrate one's ministry.

Smeeth church appears to be a combination of genuine Norman and pseudo Norman building. It is the tower that is the latter having been erected in a restoration in 1881. As a practice, it seems perfectly reasonable to me to rebuild in a style consistent with the original remnants but why then at Smeeth be satisfield with such a stunted tower; a few more feet in height would have made all the difference and earned full marks — from me at least.

The church stands in a stone-walled churchyard up a side road from the A20 to Folkestone. Mercifully for Smeeth the heavy traffic on the A20 has now been attracted away by the new, sunken M20 — so for this village progress has not been adverse. Around the churchyard are grouped comfortable, mellow houses and they must bless their new-found peace. Here, as I wandered around in the long, damp grass, I was particularly struck by the apparent absence of life. Not a soul moved; the houses could have been abandoned and deserted and, except that the time was noon, it was rather like Gray's Elegy. Presumably everyone was out at work and the children at school somewhere. So much for increasing leisure and three million unemployed — of these I was the only representative.

The church is notable for its association with the prominent families who have lived nearby. The first, chronologically, were the Scotts (now extinct locally). Their line traced back to that Balliol who was briefly King of Scotland and who founded Balliol College at Oxford. A later Scott took charge of 3500 men, mustered at Smeeth, to repel a Kent landing by the Spanish Armada. It reminds one forcibly of the Home Guard, 350 years on. The Scotts lived at Scotts' Hall, an immense mansion in the parish, now demolished, but one of its ancient oak doors survives to do duty as the church door within the weatherboarded south porch and some of the Hall's panelling, date marked 1615, graces the interior. The door was rescued from the bottom of a pond and the panelling found in a farmhouse; one might conclude that the present generation is better at preserving relics than can have been our predecessors.

A more recent patrician family linked to the church is that of the Knatchbulls. They seem to have divided their association between Smeeth and Mersham. Mersham is a couple of miles away on the far side of the M20 and was my second subject on the day I drew Smeeth. One should take notes of points of interest at the time; I failed to and now have difficulty in remembering whether this feature or that curiosity belonged to Smeeth or Mersham. For the Knatchbulls the problem must have been more acute — which church to attend on a Sunday morning; which church to support financially and so on. They seem to have come down more on the side of Mersham leaving Smeeth plainer internally but with its austere Norman features less overlaid by subsequent embellishment.

Mersham church is well known to the cognoscenti for its extraordinary west window and for the Knatchbull family memorials. The window, which dates from the end of the 14th century, is large for a country church, semi-circular and looks as if it suffers from schizophrenia, the stone tracery of the lower half being Perpendicular, the upper half Decorated in style. Since the window can hardly have been constructed at different periods of time, one can only assume that the masons received conflicting instructions from more than one master. The coats of arms of local families were incorporated in its stained glass and their various wishes at the time might account for the variations of style. As an explanation of an eccentric and arresting design that is probably naive and incorrect but it satisfies my amateur theorising. The church is placed close the west boundary of its churchyard and consequently one is frustrated by lack of distance from attempting a sketch of the window; probably just as well as the tracery would certainly not be easy to reproduce. Photography is not similarly inhibited.

The Knatchbull memorials are handsome and numerous, the south chapel being entirely devoted to them. As competition there are two small brasses, now vertically secured to the chancel wall, and a tiny tablet by the 'first English sculptor of repute'; so tiny I failed to find it. The whole chapel, indeed the church as well, is redolent of the past and of those who were prominent in the county in their day. We are not so sure of ourselves nowadays and I expect that future generations will regret our present tendency to monumental anonymity. There is little contemporary display for future historical interest and our churches will be the duller as a consequence.

The church, as my drawing attempts to show, is a fine, substantial medieval building. It seems extravangantly large for the village which has now become, I would imagine, a dormitory for the expanded town of Ashford. It is curious that apart from Court Lodge, against the churchyard wall, all the houses in the immediate vicinity are modern and they do seem incongruous. The period houses in the village are elsewhere; one supposes that there must have been considerable demolition and property development in the recent past for the church's neighbours to be so anachronistic. This modernisation continues. The church notes end their commentary with a self-congratulatory statement that a kitchenette and toilets have been added to the north vestry. I may be altogether mistaken but I can't help feeling that kitchenettes and toilets add little to the magic of an old church or to the mystery of its religion. People will come to see architecture and memorials; I doubt if they will come to see kitchenettes.

WALLTHAM
St. Bartholomew

Forest settlement

Waltham church can never have been important in the diocesan league tables. The hamlet is now not much more than a clutch of houses and a pub at a cross roads, high on the Downs south of Canterbury. The church itself marks the limit of habitation and, beyond, the land falls away to empty fields and woods. It seems like an outpost in unsettled territory and perhaps that is what it once was.

As a building the church is simple with pre-medieval overtones. There is a fairly substantial nave separated from a small chancel by a rectangular central tower. Both the north and south entrances are now blocked, the north porch, if there ever was one, has disappeared and the south one is open to the wind and weather. It has become the haunt of spiders and other creepy-crawlies; I did not venture to examine it too closely. In the absence of conventional entrances, one gains access through that flint and brick 'bus shelter' under the west window. Inside, a lobby, from which stairs lead to a musicians' gallery, acts as a sort of anteroom to the ample nave. Its size suggests a larger population when the church was built in the early centuries after the Norman occupation than there is today on these windswept Downs. An atmosphere of religious secrecy is strongly conveyed by the small chancel arch beyond the 13th century pillars which support the central tower. The impression one obtains is that the authorities did not wish the mysteries they celebrated in the chancel to be too visibly exposed to, the peasant congregation in the nave. If unquestioning faith is to be maintained, such an emphasis on mystery seems to me to be a sound policy; attempts to explain the unexplainable can easily lead to scepticism and loss of adherents as is possibly the case in our churches today. That is why the romantic and arcane latin language is such a potent ally of religious faith; what a mistake it is to make the services so comprehensible that they begin to seem trite and implausible.

Externally the walls of the church are of flint, rendered with patches of faded and crumbling cement. Where repairs have been necessary, as on the tower, and in the newer south buttresses, brick has been used and this combination of discoloured rendering, flint and brick creates a most agreeable mosaic effect. Despite its age and isolation, the church and its churchyard are not neglected; the grass was cut where it needed to be, a new, small, oaken gate, designed to repeat the stone tracery of the west window facing it, has been installed in the low, flint churchyard wall and the notices were up to date. There are octogenarian yews, a representative muster of headstones, two iron crosses and the rolling unspoilt Downs about. Waltham is an oasis that has survived the passage of the centuries and the onset of modern civilisation unscathed; happily it has been spared the attentions of Victorian restorers and I cannot imagine any occasion for its peaceful sleep in the future to be any less undisturbed than it would seem to have been in the past.

156

Petham church stands on a hillside overlooking its village which nestles peacefully below in a small downland valley above the Great Stour. It is a pocket of Kent that leads to nowhere and benefits accordingly from lack of modern development and road traffic; perhaps the presence of the Roman road, Stone Street, which runs past, from Canterbury South towards Hythe, may help to keep the traffic at bay.

The church is 13th century, or rather was, until a disastrous fire, on Sunday 26th May 1922, burnt out everything except the walls, the floor and the stone memorials. A Sunday does seem an unfortunate day for a church fire and takes rather more theological explanation than would a weekday fire. But there it was, the fire took place and the church had to be rebuilt or abandoned. Rebuilt it was and very well too.

The restoration started with advantage of a splendid floor of grey flags and ledger stones; I can't remember seeing a church floor so free of Victorian retiling and so appropriate for its purpose. Next the roof. This had to be entirely replaced and, in doing so, the opportunity was taken to decorate the new roof beams and carve and paint their supporting corbels. Super it all looks and one can almost feel grateful for the fire. Similarly the pews. Before the fire, these were plain apparently, but in 1969, reproductions of 16th century pews, all identical and with carved poppy-head bench ends, were brought from Norfolk — Norfolk's loss, I would say.

Of the memorials, the ones that I remember are three enigmatic stone coffin lids which have been fixed vertically to the interior walls of the tower and, in the churchyard, a length of timber, supported horizontally on two uprights, bearing the inscription 'Journey's End'; those words make an exact and conclusive epitaph but no doubt the faithful might prefer to assert 'Journey's Beginning'. At all events, it struck more of a chord with me than those extravagant eulogies that one sees recorded on the hanging monuments around many chancel walls.

Petham church is difficult to draw; too long broadside on, too obscured end on. On such occasions, one feels that those who planted the churchyard yews might have paid more attention to the needs of artistic representation but what an unjust and ungrateful thought. Without the efforts of the builders, the planters and the deceased to grace the surroundings there would be no elegiac churches to sketch and wonder at. Instead there would be a forlorn vacuum in the countryside of which everyone, believer or agnostic, consciously or unconsciously, would be aware. One should learn to accept with a good grace such minor obstacles as an intrusive yew and be thankful for what we have. I am.

CRUNDALE
St. Mary

Chalk pit

It is difficult to understand why Crundale church is where it is, high on a ridge of the Wye Downs. The miniature village lies below in the valley and one cannot see many of today's parishioners struggling up the hill to attend the services; no doubt when the church was built they were better walkers, they had to be, and climbers too, but they must perforce have elected to live in the valley where the springs emerge. On top it is beautiful but bare and empty of life apart from the ubiquitous birds. Pheasants foraged around, quite unruffled by my questing presence; they would not even take wing for a stone lobbed in their direction.

The church, modest in size, is largely made of flint and has Norman origins although of course there have been later additions and modifications. Structurally it is relatively unusual in having its unbuttressed tower midway along the north face; and with a heavily buttressed west gable end to the nave. The flint work is a lesson in developing masonry practice; the oldest part being rough and ready, the later construction being that of neat, squared, close-set knapped flints which provides a sounder, if less visually evocative, wall for load bearing purposes. There is, as well, from a more recent restoration, a pattern of grey and black chequered squares at the peak of the chancel's gable end; very effective it looks too.

Inside, one's attention is immediately attracted by a substantial tomb chest, the alabaster lid of which is decorated with a life-size figure of John Sprot, a priest who died in 1466. He lies there, as he has for the last 500 years, in the small, cell-like, west end of the afterthought north nave. One wonders what John Sprot achieved in his life to have secured such posthumous immortality. Imagine, if you can, what the world will be like should you be similarly immortalised for the next 500 years; it defies my imagination and yet I can see no reason why John Sprot should not remain undisturbed where he is until the slow geological change finally obliterates the Downs. In the nave itself there is further evidence of permanence. Three immense ledger stones lie on the floor of the aisle between the pews. One in particular, of black slate, commemorates the Carter family who lived and died in the mid 1600s — 300 years ago. No-one who visits Crundale church can possibly overlook Geo. Carter, Gent, which must be precisely what he intended all those years ago. That does convey an admirable air of confidence in the immutability of things.

When I was there, the visitors book was opened and showed that a page and a half had been filled with names in the preceeding twelve days, that is roughly twenty five to thirty families had visited the church, including five from overseas. It is a remarkable stream of traffic considering how isolated and unpretentious is the little church. I had difficulty in finding it, aloof from its village, and it was only when I followed a signpost to 'Sole Street Church' that I realised that I was in fact being led to Crundale church. Assuredly that is one way of preserving privacy from all except the persevering but one can't help feeling that such reticence can hardly be what either John Sprot's or George Carter's executors had in mind when they commissioned those memorials for the deceased.

160

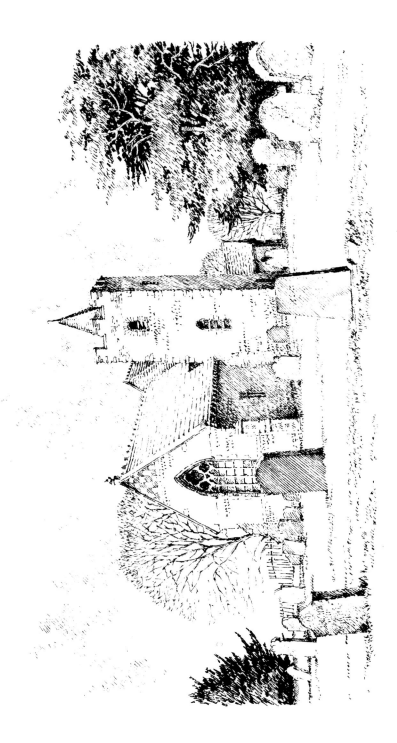

LUDDENHAM
St. Mary

Luda's settlement

None of my favourite authorities have much to say about Luddenham church. Arthur Mee dismisses it in one brief derogatory sentence, Pevsner with little more and Charles Igglesden, in his thirty odd volumes of a 'Saunter through Kent with Pen and Pencil' ignores it altogether. Hasted and his imitator, Ireland, do briefly mention a feud between the lord of the manor and Canterbury over the advowson of the church in the reign of King John but otherwise the church has lived in obscurity and anonymity.

It is not surprising. Today the church stands, locked, redundant and lifeless, on the edge of the Swale marshes. There is no village, never has been, so why the church is where it is at all is a mystery. In place of a village, there is Luddenham Court and its attendant farm buildings which entirely enclose the church and churchyard. The quarter mile road to the church and farm is marked 'Private' but I could not accept that a road to a church could be so designated and I ignored the prohibition. Arrived at the church, there were further warnings about 'Trespassers' and to 'Beware of the dogs'. Grouped around were the barns, untidy with sacks of fertiliser, bales of straw and idle farm machinery but not a soul stirred. It was unexpected and unwelcoming and I felt reluctant to leave the security of my car parked by the churchyard wall.

Eventually I did — cautiously, as one does not want to meet all alone, a truculent guard dog on his home ground even if it is, or was, hallowed. The low, surrounding wall was in reasonable repair but the small gate in a state of collapse; the churchyard was untended and overshadowed by the encircling ring of tall lime trees; the porch door padlocked and evidently long disused. Architecturally the church is not exciting but its nave and chancel are medieval. The square, brick tower and plain little porch are Victorian and what possessed someone to put up such a tower in 1807 defies reason when one reads in Hasted that the houses of the parish numbered only ten in 1780. It is an extravagant expenditure for a micro congregation. Structurally the church looked sound, no tiles missing from the roof and the windows secure, so upkeep has not been lacking in the past. Now it must face a future of slow disintegration.

At midday, with no-one about in the middle of a prosperous farmstead, I felt vaguely uneasy and tended to keep a watchful eye over my shoulder as I sketched. At night, when what farm workers there are have gone home, the owls are hooting in the limes, and the lapwings are mewing on the marsh, I would imagine that the owners of Luddenham Court could feel the presence of the abandoned church pressing on their spirits. Liking old country churches as I do, I nonetheless did not envy Luddenham Court the captive relic in its midst and I was not sorry to finish my trespass.

162

Oare village stands at the head of one of the two substantial creeks that extend inland from the Swale towards Faversham. It is not beautiful and Pevsner describes it as 'dour'. I suppose there is a somewhat economy look to it but that simplicity probably reflects the depressed conditions between the wars when most of the houses were built. I don't think the same thing applies today. There is a large, active factory on the far side of the creek, which, in November, was crowded with yachts and boats laid up for the winter. As everyone knows yachting does not come cheap so there can be little or no financial stringency at Oare today — rather the reverse. The Three Mariners, the comfortable pub at which I had one expensive sandwich repeated this present prosperity and was appropriately up-market in decor and bar prices.

Times have changed for Oare. How that has affected the church is not clear. This stands at the seaward limit of the village on a bank overlooking its rival distraction, the creek. From the road there is a misleading suggestion of a dark Victorian building. This impression is due to the west tower which confronts one and which seven sons caused to be erected in memory of their mother in 1877; prior to that the church could only run to a bellcote. Apart from the Victorian tower, the church consists of a 16th century nave extending without interruption into the chancel. The discerning, or those informed by Pevsner, can identify by the embedded quoin stones, where these two elements of the church are mated. Great is the satisfaction to be gained from prior intelligence.

The church was locked; but no memorials are mentioned by Pevsner so I doubt if I missed anything of note although this little church could well harbour the remains of some who fought the Dutch at Camperdown or hurled abuse at them when they raided the Medway up to Chatham in 1667. I expect that Oare has always produced its quota of seamen but perhaps, like their village, they were of insufficient worldly consequence to qualify for grand memorials.

Leaving aside these speculations and the unseen interior, Oare church must enjoy one of the better sites in the county. Immediately to the east of the chancel the ground falls steeply to the level of the creek and thence stretches away with little distraction to the outer reaches of the Thames estuary. The churchyard takes in the decline to the marsh and sporadic tombstones maintain their positions uneasily on the slope; I had a similar problem while I attempted my sketch. For those who attend the services, the church's situation, perched on its old raised beach, must provide one of the rare instances when opaque stained glass windows are regretted by the congregation. But in the 1980s, I suspect that most of the potential congregation are less concerned, being down on the creek in their boats on Sundays. And that is very likely the change that material prosperity has brought to Oare church in the 20th century.

BOUGHTON-UNDER-BLEAN
St. Peter and St. Paul

Charter farmstead

St. Peter and St. Paul, at Boughton-under-Blean, the fourth Boughton church in Kent, is fortunate that both the broad swathe of the M2 motorway and its Roman predecessor, the Watling Street from Canterbury, give it a wide berth and leave it in peace amongst the orchards and hopfields. Its village, for some reason called Boughton Street, also keeps well clear and only three period houses, to represent the Blean, keep the church company on its windy ridge. However isolation has not meant neglect in the case of St. Peter and St. Paul.

Far from it. When I arrived to make my sketch, I found the church in a state of turmoil and disarray. Externally, the crowded and oddly-shaped churchyard was cluttered with builders' materials, huts, etc; ladders and scaffolding encumbered the fabric and canvas flapped on the roofs where tiles should be. Inside, Radio 2 blared fortissimo and practically everything, including the three screens and pulpit, was covered in protective cellophane against the all-pervading dust. All this unseemly, but purposeful, chaos arouse, I gathered, from an extensive and no doubt costly re-roofing; surprising when one reads in Pevsner that there was a restoration campaign in 1871. They can't have been too thorough then but they did only spend £2,000. Even in 1871 £2,000 can't have gone very far.

This 13th century flint church manifestly deserves the care and expense presently devoted to its upkeep. The plaster on the internal walls has been carefully stripped away from the stone surrounds of the Decorated and Perpendicular period windows and this practice, I find, creates a most agreeable interior effect. The church is also exceptionally well-endowed with monuments, the most elaborate of which is a large stone table tomb, surmounted by the alabaster effigies of a 17th century knight and his long-suffering wife, and bordered by a carved frieze of their seven adult sons and six daughters. This tomb alone, sculpted by the famous Epiphanius Evesham, must be important enough to guarantee the proper maintenance of the church, and it is curious to reflect that what could once have been considered an ostentatious extravagance now more than pays the rent for the space it occupies.

When the builders' men (and the bellringer who had come along to cast an anxious eye on the work in progress) left for their lunch, I was given their encouragement to ascend the tower's spiral staircase. I have a very unreasonable aversion to heights and a few circuits of that narrow, steep, stone spiral was too much for me and I cravenly retired from a rare opportunity to survey the east Kent countryside from such an eerie. Very probably the towers of Canterbury cathedral would have been well in sight and that alone should have persuaded me to persevere with that claustrophobic stair turret. Unfortunately not so; from the security of my study, I can now regret an original, if exposed, perspective for my sketch — missed through an innate phobia of heights.

Selling church is described as 'interesting' by more than one authority but none has anything very interesting to record about it. As the porch was locked and I couldn't get in, my comments will be equally uninformative; I was sorry though to miss the flag flown at Trafalgar which apparently is displayed therein.

Well away from its straggling village, itself a rural rarity in possessing a railway station, the church stands in a particularly attractive cul de sac of a country lane. The domed churchyard, retained above the encircling roadway by a well-found flint wall, looks out on three or four houses, empty fields and the foothills of the North Downs. There is no suggestion of anything so prosaic as a railway in sight.

The church is flint, Early English, and furnished with a north and south chapel, a north and south aisle to the nave, west and south porches, a north transept and the whole assembly, not large although it may sound so, topped off with a central, stuccoed tower. If one could ignore the unfortunate but doubtless necessary stucco, it would make a very harmonious group on the crown of its churchyard lawn. I fear I may have been too distracted by the flint retaining wall to do justice to the church.

Exploring so many country churches as I do, I can't help becoming aware of a change in our social conventions. From Tudor to Victorian times people seemed anxious to assert their earthly, rather than religious, status by the grandeur of their memorials and the churches and churchyards benefited accordingly. Society no longer seeks such permanent, and often beautiful, status symbols. A case in point is Winston Churchill's inconspicuous memorial at Blagdon — quite inappropriate, I would maintain, to someone of his historic importance. Selling churchyard is no exception. I saw no recent memorial to rival that commanding Victorian plinth in the foreground of my sketch. The status symbols of today are, or were, motor cars and expensive foreign holidays; certainly ephemeral, and I suspect that a solid stone memorial will prove more satisfying in the long run to future generations than immediate, self-centred, consumption leaving nothing behind. Perhaps the arrival of the nuclear age has caused a loss of confidence in the future — but then isn't the future what the Church is supposed to be all about?

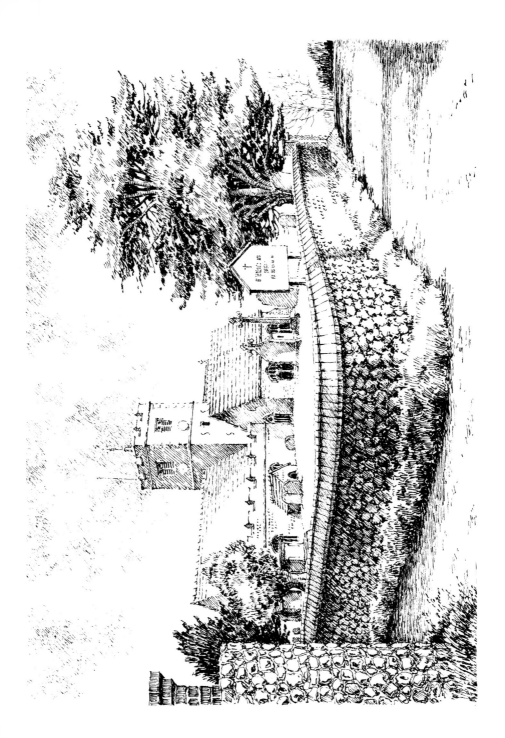

CUXTON
St. Michael

Cucula's stone

Cuxton village, on the north bank of the Medway, almost opposite Rochester, must be a very ancient settlement but you wouldn't think so today. Despite its Saxon origins, it consists of a, no doubt, comfortable, but visually unexciting, 20th century housing complex compressed between the Downs and the river. In 1760, Cuxton boasted ninety three inhabitants; now there are some 2,000, so it is not surprising that little remains of the past. Except the church that is, perched high above the main road and dominating the river below.

From the excellent church booklet, one learns of the discovery of pre-historic flint hand axes in the vicinity, macabre burials, Roman tiles and pottery, and a Saxon church on the site prior to the existing building. This latter is mainly a combination of the Norman and Perpendicular periods with minor 19th century additions which do not enjoy entirely unqualified admiration. It is not a large church but very solidly built of flint and stone and unless it descends to the river, it looks good for another millenium.

Apart from its commanding, and happily now by-passed, position looking across the Medway, Cuxton church's claims to fame must rely on its local pre-history and on its illustrious, but unfortunate and unbending, rector for a few months in 1610, William Laud, later Archbishop of Canterbury and victim of Parliamentary revenge. How he must have regretted his advancement from the obscurity of Cuxton as he waited for the relatively merciful axe on the scaffold in 1645.

An oddity of the church is its SE/NW axis. This unorthodox line-up places it at right angles to the river but, at the same time, takes the east end of the chancel perilously close to the edge of the plateau on which the church rests. Probably its builders were following the line of earlier Saxon foundations, or alternatively perhaps they could not resist such a dramatic orientation on the slope of the Downs; I prefer the latter hypothesis which is my own.

It was paralysingly cold when I attempted my sketch looking down on the church from a neglected copse above the churchyard. Like the church, I faced south east across the river from whence a Siberian wind blew without hindrance. After half an hour I could stand it no more and retreated before my bones became set in permafrost. Surprisingly enough, there was a lot of activity around the church that December day; a gardener was tidying the already immaculate churchyard and some others were clearing the scrub at the east entrance to the churchyard to make a picnic area. Their work allowed, indeed required, a bonfire and I was suitably envious. Stoking a bonfire had a distinct advantage over sitting still with a pen in a shaking hand in arctic conditions but then the workers were at it all day whereas I was only a bird of passage on that winter morning.

170

Meopham has not been the luckiest of my church forays. On the first occasion on which I attempted a sketch, it came on to rain before I could record anything worth reproduction at home; on the second it was so cold that the weakness of the flesh prevailed and I was obliged to seek refuge in the nearest pub and, on the third and final attempt, I found that I had inadvertently brought my note pad instead of my drawing pad. Malediction — but I couldn't be defeated for a third time so the writing pad was pressed into service and to my surprise proved reasonably adequate for a rough preliminary sketch.

Meopham village does not really deserve its church. The former now amounts to an untidy and elongated straggle of ribbon development lining the A227 as it runs along the crown of the North Downs between Wrotham and Gravesend. Meopham has lost its one-time rural identity and become something of a commuter village and, in its present condition, is a convincing argument for town and country planning.

But the church is in a different category. It is a substantial flint building, reinforced by grey stone at the corners and repaired here and there by mellow brick work. Apparently the fabric was completely rebuilt in 1325 and, to judge from the meticulous, close-set, squared flint work, expense was not a limiting factor. No doubt such good fortune arose from the election of a native of Meopham, Simon, to the throne of Canterbury in 1328. Incidentally, the church guide remarks that Simon had to raise a loan to defray the costs of travelling to Avignon for his consecration so possibly the church builders had to wait a year or two for settlement. Now a similar situation prevails; a rescue fund of £80,000 is needed, of which only £40,000 has so far been subscribed. In Simon's day, there was no need of a public appeal for funds; instead indulgences could be, and were, sold to all who visited the church. Optimistic appeals to a non-religious community for money in the 20th century seem a less sure way of raising capital than did the sale of indulgences to a credulous population, and if nothing else, the church authorities of the 14th century were clearly financial realists. They cannot have been thorough in their exactions, though, as the discovery in 1973 of a hidden hoard of fourteen gold coins, dating from the reigns of Edward III and Richard II, would suggest.

Nevertheless, compared to many other village churches in Kent, St. John the Baptist looks to be in better condition and less in need of rescue than, for instance, its immediate neighbours of Nurstead and Luddesdown. They have little or no village to call on; Meopham, with a population of over 7,000, has almost outgrown its village status and exchanged unspoilt fields for financial muscle. I dare say Simon de Meopham would have approved.

GREAT CHART
St. Mary the Virgin

When it was originally built by the Normans, the church at Great Chart was prominently placed to command its parish from the crest of a small hill. Now the expanding town of Ashford looms menacingly close and the traffic between Tenterden and Ashford streams incessantly past the churchyard gate. The commanding eminence is diminished but they are making a by-pass to the east of the village and this will provide much needed relief to the church and to the villagers and, at least, restore the former rural tranquillity.

It is a handsome church of Kentish ragstone exhibiting to the passer-by the typical level east front of chancel and supporting chapels. The history of the church is confused, I find. Originally Norman, it was completely rebuilt in the 14th century, reason not clear, and then badly damaged by fire in the 15th century. Fortunately a native son of Great Chart had by then become Bishop of Norwich and he obtained permission from Rome to grant indulgences to pay for repairs. Whatever theological or ethical objections there may be, there is no doubt that indulgences were a most effective way of raising money. Equally any church benefited greatly from a powerful local patron like James Goldwell of Great Chart or Simon of Meopham. I would imagine that almost every country church owes its survival to some well-placed benefactor. It is an argument for privilege.

Great Chart possesses one curiosity and one architectural conundrum. The conundrum concerns the junction between the nave and chancel, normally defined by the chancel arch. At Great Chart the arch is some way into the nave. I suppose the rebuilding in 1472 must account for this anomaly. Another peculiarity, to my mind, concerns the buttresses which support the east end of the chancel. So placed, their angle to the front of the chancel would suggest that the north and south chapels were later additions. But in fact the church history and guide claims that the south chapel is the oldest part of the present building; it would be impertinent of me to question the official guide so the angle of the offending buttresses must remain unexplained.

The curiosity concerns that minute 16th century building beside the churchyard gate. It is variously described as the pest house, the priest's house, and the gate house. Its uses have been equally various; excluding an asylum for victims of the plague, which is unlikely, the little house has apparently been used as the residence of the priest, a place of business for the churchwardens, the sexton's house, somewhere for the Sunday School and for the Girl Guides. Although not much larger than a good-sized, one-car garage, it must be a versatile building to have provided accommodation for such diverse activities for so long. It is most attractive and, in its own way, as great a treasure as the medieval parish church to which it is attached.

HIGH HALDEN
St. Mary

Heaouweald's woodland pasture

The outstanding feature, one cannot call it the redeeming feature of this Weald church, is its extraordinary belfry tower. This is made entirely of wood from the topmost point of its steeple to the foot of its octagonal, expanded base. The effect is Scandinavian and unlike that of any church in Kent that I have explored so far.

The tower was built in the reign of Henry VIII (pace Hasted who contends the reign of Henry VI) when High Halden was surrounded by woodland and fifty tons of the best timber, it is said, went into the construction of this eccentric belfry. Inside the base of the tower which serves as porch and bellringers' chamber, a framed notice refers one to the Archaeologia Cantiana, volume twenty six of the Society's Proceedings, for details of its design; obediently therefore and without undue delay I reported to the local Tonbridge public library for further enlightenment. Public libraries today are excellent and I find the reference section at Tonbridge a constant source of pleasure and information; that it is free to the relatively few users seems to me an irresponsible exercise of their stewardship by the Council over their ratepayers' subscriptions. However I ride a hobby horse and digress. Volume twenty six lived up to my expectations; High Halden church and its wooden tower was described in 1904 in a lengthy essay by the Rev. G.M. Livett FSA. I could not help being impressed by his learning and attention to every last detail. There must have been time to spare in 1904 for a vicar of Wateringbury to have unearthed such a mass of information about one small church, to have laboriously committed it to paper and for the reader to read it. We are not so thorough today.

As I have become more aware of the enormous reference potential available in public libraries I begin to realise that the unscrupulous, or lazy, could well compile an informed guide-book without ever leaving the comfort of the reference section of the library. Could it be that this is what is often done?

More attractive than the steeple, and older being 14th century, is the now unused south porch which I have drawn in preference to a more conventional rendering of High Halden. Inside, the church's somewhat uninteresting and plain appearance was notable, so far as I was concerned, only for the enlarged circular marble bases to each of the arcade pillars; stone seats according to Arthur Mee — the stumps of an earlier 13th century arcade suggests Pevsner; I expect the Rev. Livett has the right of it in his learned article. But really, apart from the south porch, the church at High Halden depends for its local and ecclesiological renown on its remarkable west tower. My drawing makes no concession to this aspect and, to that extent, inadequately conveys the unique impression that this church must make on any visitor. I admit that any picture should identify its subject without question; I have not done so and must plead the 14th century south porch as my defence.

176

SHELDWICH
St. James

Shield Farm

In today's congested conditions the church at Sheldwich is no longer happily placed, bordering, as it does, the Faversham—Ashford road with only a narrow pavement separating the churchyard wall from the relentless traffic. There is no side road and nowhere to park so what happens on Sundays I cannot imagine. As it was I had to park some way away in a disused farmyard and my sketch was undertaken in a state of anxiety for the safety of my car in my absence. The church also suffers from untidy over-treeing to its south and west so that little or no sunlight reaches the building and an impression of gloom pervades. To the north and south lie open fields but viewed from this direction the church merges imperceptibly with the trees looming darkly behind. I felt that attention to the wooded south boundary of the churchyard could well relieve the shadows and would materially benefit the situation of the church.

It is an old, much restored, and architecturally unusual church, it seemed to me. The nave is substantially Norman, to quote Pevsner, with a conventional south chapel. The odd feature is that of the chancel with its discordant, shallow roof interrupting the window at the gable end of the nave. Generally the pitch of the various roofs of a church is sympathetically parallel; here the angular difference is substantial and distinct but perhaps the intention was to reveal that extraordinary 14th century window at the apex of the nave gable. Although not obvious from my drawing, it is described as a 'mouchette wheel within a sinuous triangular outline' (a mouchette my glossary tells me is a 'tracery in the shape of a curved dagger') and, according to Pevsner, is unique to Kent. It is a pity, though, that the chancel roof couldn't have been lowered a little more to expose the complete window. However one should not complain too much as apparently this gem of a window was only rediscovered in 1888 at the Victorian restoration.

The churchyard is dominated by the memorials to the Sondes family, the local grandees here and at neighbouring Throwley from the time of Charles II. At Sheldwich they have contented themselves with the close-set group of crosses plus a column and a winged angel (omitted by me); at Throwley, a better church, their ancestors built a chapel for their mausoleum and this contains, amongst other things, a pair of very handsome tomb chests considerably outranking the Sheldwich crosses. I never enjoy drawing crosses; they don't lend themselves to my pencil nor do they mellow or convey any air of antiquity. Nevertheless in the Sheldwich churchyard, the concentrated Sondes group could hardly be ignored and had to be attempted — with the results that you can see.

178

NORTON
St. Mary

I suppose what must distinguish Norton church from most other country churches is its inaccessability. My map showed roughly where I could expect to find it but there was not a sign of it from the lane near the village. At length I tried another lane leading between orchards and hopfields and suddenly I found myself passing a temporary notice propped at the side of the road at a gap in the hedge to announce the church. One approaches between the lines of apple trees along a track of beaten earth; it suggests that this unconventional entrance can only be a temporary measure but the church has been where it is at least since the 13th century and there is no other approach. Indeed the picket fence around the churchyard makes it clear that the orchard approach is permanent; it must be the orchard which is the interloper and which has absorbed the traditional path to the church from the hidden village. The fruit trees are newish, restricted in the modern habit so that cultivation and harvesting are simplified and made less labour intensive. I wonder how it was that the road to the church could have been appropriated for commercial fruit production.

As might be expected, the doors were locked. The church is modest in size, consisting of a simple nave and chancel with a plain, square tower at the west end. The walls are of flint, partly rendered with mottled and crumbling cement and the tower has been reinforced by one solitary, diagonal buttress and with Victorian brickwork at its corners. The church is fortunate in the possession of an elegant row of five identical 14th century lancet windows to light the nave and chancel and these do cheer up a somewhat unambitious exterior. According to Pevsner, though, the monuments inside more than compensate for the lack of distinction outside and I was sorry to miss them.

In the churchyard, however, there was one pleasant surprise for a retired naval officer. Close by the gate on that tall prominent cross, was a clearly decipherable epitaph to one Francis James Lindsay Blackwood. It read '. . . He was . . . the grandson of Vice Admiral the Hon. Sir Henry Blackwood, Bart., K.C.B., G.G.H., (who was the bearer of the despatches announcing the Victory of Trafalgar) . . .' If I remember correctly from the 'Sea Kings of Britain', on which we were reared at Dartmouth as budding naval officers, Blackwood was one of Nelson's captains and it was he who anchored his ship off the shoals of Aboukir Bay to act as a navigational mark for Nelson and the fleet as they swept down to destroy the sheltering French fleet. I felt the brush of history and a reminder of my departed youth from that silent memorial in the deserted churchyard. It made my day.

Poor little Iwade church; it deserves better than its present depressing surround-ings. It lies immediately beside the busy main road just before one reaches the modern Kingsferry bridge which provides access to industrial Sheppey beyond the River Swale. Sheerness, in Sheppey, no longer a minor Georgian naval dockyard, has become a thriving import/export link with the Low Countries and the evidence for this thunders dangerously through what is left of Iwade. There is no need for the pre-occupied traffic to stop for there is nothing now worth seeing at Iwade except the hidden church. This, at least, has some exceedingly plain cottages for protection from the articulated trucks; behind it, a sort of untidy 'fell-off-the-back-of-a-lorry' small-holding completes the ignoble encirclement. There must have been a village of sorts once at Iwade to justify a 14th century church but nothing today remains that is remotely attractive or honourably ancient; I don't think I am being unfair to Iwade but I trust that no-one from that village reads this. It seems unlikely.

With Iwade hamlet such a non-event, the medieval church has been spared restoration and appears to be essentially the original 14th century building plus a Victorian south porch. The construction is mainly of rubble stone apart from the squat west tower which is of flint. There was once a west door but this is now blocked and all that survives are traces of the primitive gothic arrangement of the voussoir stones framing the one-time entrance. Above are two tiny lancet windows which look no younger or any more regular than the voussoirs below. The Victorian porch, which shelters the antique church door proper, firmly padlocked against the visitor, is also of flint and looks largely untouched by the weather. The rest of the fabric, though, is beautifully mellowed, and to use an antique dealer's term 'dis-tressed'; the drop stones above the Perpendicular windows have crumbled in part, the roof tiles are rosy-red, splintered and slipping, the torching under these tiles is missing in places and the north wall of the nave is belling outwards uncertainly. Externally, therefore, it is a simple and unaffected little church but if only its surroundings weren't so awful. Magic away what presumes to call itself the village of Iwade and you would have this church surrounded by fields of pasture, sweeping marshes, the Swale and the low hump of Sheppey beyond. It would then be a landscape for which the church could have been, and very likely was, designed and the one would enhance the other. One could make a pilgrimage there — as I suppose, in a way, I could be said to have done in my secular exploration.

QUEENBOROUGH
Holy Trinity

Queenborough does not properly qualify as a country church but, having berthed my M.T.B. at Queenborough jetty for one night towards the end of the war, I have always felt I owed the port a return visit.

The town in fact is nowhere near the jetty and I saw nothing of it then. It is really an historic little place having been founded by the warrior Plantagenet, Edward III when he built a castle there as a defence against the French maritime raids up the Thames via the Swale in the days of the Hundred Years War. Nothing of the castle now remains but the church, built at roughly the same date in 1366, is still very much in evidence in the heart of an apparently rejuvenated town. It had obviously become a run-down backwater with little to recall its royal foundation but, with the collapse of the London docks, modest ports like Queenborough have stepped in to scoop the business thrown away up river. Queenborough now looks to me as if commercial activity, and presumably prosperity too, have returned to salvage the fortunes of the port and this must be good for the parish church.

Externally the church appears rather dark and unexciting. The tower and its turret are said to be original but all the windows on the south side of the nave, facing me as I drew, were renewed in the 1880s. They all now match each other, even to the dormer window, and present a uniform, if undramatic, facade to front the high street. Notwithstanding its origins the church at Queenborough is democratically upstaged by the churchyard with its massed ranks of gravestones. I can't remember a churchyard so well stocked, if that is an appropriate expression for a graveyard. The piece de resistance is, of course, that prominent obelisk erected by the Greet family to proclaim their status. The inscriptions on it are still legible and I was intrigued by the contrast between the first epitaph in 1798, to a child aged six weeks, and the most recent in 1947, to an Admiral Greet aged 93. Another inscription which aroused my interest was that to a captain who served 'under the King of Sweeden' (sic). I am sure that there are many more curiosities to be deciphered in that churchyard had one the time and persistence to uncover them.

I can't forbear one word of criticism. On the north side of the church, amongst the lesser headstones, there stands a corrugated-iron shed, for the Scouts I believe, but its presence next the nave is an act of vandalism by the church authorities. How they can be so iconoclastic and oblivious of the past defeats me. I don't doubt that, if they could, all those buried so reverently and memorialised so confidently in that crowded churchyard, would rise up and spirit away the unworthy anachronism. I took care to do my sketch on the far south side of the church; I would not like to insult a 14th century building with a 20th century tin shack on the same page.

Wrotham has an impressive church for so small a village but I suppose it is not to be wondered at when one remembers that there is the remnant of an Archbishop's palace alongside the churchyard. Whether those early Archbishops would be so pleased with Wrotham's present situation is open to doubt; its site on the south slope of the Downs above Ightham remains the same but now the M20 climbs Wrotham Hill behind the church and the M25/M26 below effectively seal off the village from the Weald and the rest of Kent. So, trapped by motorways, perhaps Wrotham and its church will be preserved undeveloped and unchanged like a fly in amber.

The church is a substantial, squarish 13th century building, notable in three respects. First the west tower, which abuts the village street, has had a passage driven through at ground level, apparently to allow processions of the faithful to encircle the church without leaving the churchyard. Next, there is inside, in front of the chancel rood screen, a collection of brasses, exposed and unprotected on their ledger stones. I am not a particular fan of brasses but they do antedate headstones by about 200 years and are important for recording the fashions of their day. Here at Wrotham, I counted four sets of man and wife, two singletons and three groups of children — all at the mercy of our feet. It says something for the confidence of the vicar and churchwardens. The third jewel in the crown of Wrotham is its south porch, an imposing two storied entrance with a room above, a boss on the porch ceiling displaying the arms of the Peckham family (they of the brasses) and a bronze statue of St. George (he of the dedication) confronting all who approach by the path from the gate.

This church is attractive from whatever angle one views it. I chose the south front but regretted passing over the north face. It often seems to me that the northern aspects of many churches are more evocative than the southern, perhaps because they are generally unfrequented and have escaped renewal and updating.

Wrotham has had some ecclesiastically important rectors and vicars in the past. One came to have the dubious distinction of preaching (offensively, says Mee) at the burning of Cranmer. Let us hope he had long left Wrotham when he was called upon for that sad duty. Like many other incumbents advanced to higher ranks he would have done better, I think, to have remained with his beautiful, country church in harmless and unharming obscurity.

TROTTISCLIFFE
St. Peter and St. Paul

I have always particularly liked Trottiscliffe church (pronounced Trossley for ease); not for its architecture but for its idyllic situation at the foot of the Downs above West Malling. It lies well to the east of its village, alone except for a farmyard and an adjoining, handsome farmhouse and with a pleasant stone and weatherboarded cottage for balance. Facing the churchyard are two massive chestnut trees and beyond, to the south, the land falls away to the distant ragstone ridge which connects Sevenoaks with Maidstone. It is a harmonious group in which the ancient church makes no concession to the necessity for any parish within sight.

The church is tiny, consisting of an aisleless Norman nave and chancel which together are no larger than twice the size of my sitting room, if that. There is also a 12th century south west tower through which one enters the church; no separate porch. Inside, the small spare nave is furnished with a complete set of box pews — you don't often see that — and a surprisingly elaborate carved pulpit. The explanation for the presence of this sumptuous pulpit in humble Trottiscliffe is that, on becoming surplus to requirements at Westminster Abbey, it was surreptitiously spirited down here in 1824 by the Abbey Surveyor — an example of ecclesiological nepotism or a case of 'I didn't think anybody wanted it'.

The church also boasts, displayed in a glass-fronted cabinet, a pre-historic skull. I don't know why it should be there but, not far away, there is the neolithic sepulchre known as Coldrum Stones and probably the skull came from that pagan to this hallowed place. Whether its owner would be happy with the transition we shall never know but, as with the pulpit, Trottiscliffe seems to have become a resting place for extra-mural objects. I, too, would be perfectly happy to end my days there.

I cannot be alone in liking this church. On a previous visit, they were repairing the churchyard wall; on the occasion of my sketch, they were redecorating the interior which always suffers from damp. On an early occasion, before my time, they renewed the west wall of the nave using top quality, squared, knapped flint work. Before that again, the Bishop of Rochester had a summer manor where the farmhouse now stands behind those dignified, rusticated brick pillars. In terms of the Church's overall mission in Kent, such enduring care and expense can hardly be justified as economic budgeting; on the other hand, if the little church is regarded as an irreplaceable antique with pre-historic and pre-Norman associations, then the operations of the decorators today and of the masons yesterday seem entirely proper and prudent.

St. Peter's attraction and claim to fame must rest, of course, on its association with Anne Boleyn and Hever castle. An entrance to the castle grounds faces the church across a small expanse of grass; with a pair of old houses, a village school and a pub, the Henry VIII naturally, the group that makes up Hever village is complete. Were it not for the castle, there would be no inn and, one might suspect, no church but, in fact, St. Peter's is older than the castle by at least 100 years. Perhaps there was an earlier castle and perhaps there was a community of knights, men-at-arms, villeins, serfs and so on dependent on the castle to justify a church at Hever. There is no trace of them now and all the houses in the vicinity have become gentrified.

The church is an attractive building of honey-coloured sandstone, mottled with iron stains, dating from about 1300. It is of modest proportions but rescued externally from the run of the mill of its period by an elegant broached spire on the west tower and by that unusually prominent Tudor chimney stack for the fireplace in the north chapel. Inside, the feature which everyone comes to see is the great tomb chest close by the altar of Sir Thomas Bullen, Anne's father. In passing, it is a curious fact that Sir Thomas is always spelt 'Bullen' whereas his daughter invariably answers to 'Boleyn'. I know that spelling was rather erratic in Henry VIII's day but I would have thought we could have decided on an agreed version by now. The tomb displays the famous brass on its lid, good and solid it is, too, but otherwise the stonework is remarkably emaciated as if it had been exposed to the weather since 1538 instead of enjoying the protection of the sanctuary. It doesn't look as if it will survive for another 450 years, notwithstanding the restored roof over its head.

There are two other noteworthy brasses to be seen and one shadow of a stolen brass which, to judge by size, must have been in the same league as the Bullen brass. We can be thankful, I suppose, that the thieves only took one and left three; these survivors are beautifully clear and available for inspection and admiration. Whoever made the brasses at Hever was an artist and I should be very surprised if the subjects of his work were half as attractive as he has had the skill to make them out to be. I am all for improving on nature when it can do no harm and here at Hever it enriches the church and compliments the departed.

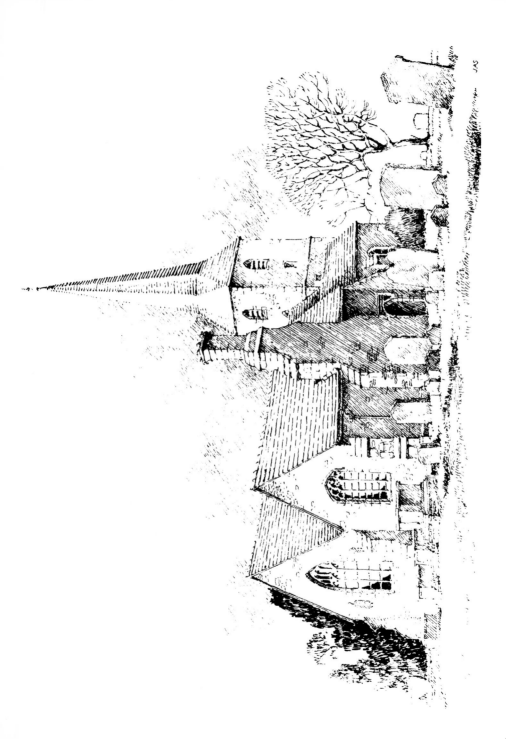

JAS

St. Mary

This very handsome 14th century church, together with a picture-postcard row of timbered houses facing it across the road, essentially makes up the village of Chiddingstone. Beyond the church and houses lies Chiddingstone Castle and park and this manifestation of 18th century landed pride effectively puts a full stop to any westward extension of the village beyond the churchyard. The whole group of church, 15th century village houses and castellated manor now make a perfectly preserved period piece and it is appropriate that, church apart, the village has been acquired by the National Trust.

One would think that the one-time lords of the manor, the Streatfeilds, owned the church but it is prior to their arrival at the castle. This impression of appropriation derives from the innumerable hanging memorials to members of the family which monopolises the interior walls; no-one else really gets a look in. There is, as well, a tomb chest to a Streatfeild wife by the altar, a 1580 brass to a Streatfeild, nine hatchments to the family, and, simplest and saddest of all, a crude, splintered, wooden cross commemorating a nineteen year old Streatfeild who died of wounds near Ypres in 1917.

My view of the church makes much of the sweeping branches of a majestic cedar and, in the foreground, the square, pyramidal vault of the Streatfeilds. To the eye, the church does not look old and this is for two reasons; first a rebuilding of the south side of the 14th century structure after a fire in 1624 and second, the smooth, unweathered appearance of the ashlared sandstone used in the repaired fabric. It looks as if it was put up yesterday. Ashlaring must be an expensive process and apparently subsidies were obtained from London, Oxford and many Kent parishes to raise the necessary £649.

When I made this drawing, it was late February with just a hint of spring in the air. Any later in the calendar and I could have been beset by tourists. I can imagine that, to many, this vignette of a village must represent the epitome of everything that they have ever dreamed about vanished rural England. The National Trust will ensure its survival unchanged and the Streatfeilds may continue undisturbed to look down from the walls in their exclusive mausoleum as they have done since 1600.

Another of those tiny downland churches, almost a chapel really, with a prosperous and busy farmstead substituting for a non-existent village. The farm possessed a herd of pedigree Ayrshires which sounded harmless enough as I sketched; there was also a pair of very aggressive geese and these eventually saw me off the premises with some loss of my dignity. In their enthusiasm they even tried to nip my car after I was safely inside.

The church consists of no more than a box-like Norman nave plus a similar, but later, chancel and two identical, but more recent still, brick porches. There was a notice inside saying that the Friends of Kent Churches were currently contributing to repairs. Just as well observing that the operational porch required a wooden frame to prevent the brick arch from collapsing. Externally the church presents an uncomplicated and unostentatious appearance. The walls are a mixture of flint, knapped and neat for the renewed chapel, crumbling, rendered and reinforced by bricks and tiles for the nave. The bellcote is diminutive and inconspicuous and the windows are few. It is an economical and unflamboyant church, both inside and out, very much as it was when designed by the Normans and the only improvements on the original are the two porches and the spirelet bellcote.

It seemed just right for its isolated situation. Here it stands, high on the Downs, in its tree-lined but empty churchyard, surrounded by a sturdy flint wall and faced by the working farm with its accompaniment of lowing cows, cackling geese and the staccato put put of the tractors. One is almost surprised that the little church has not been conscripted into the farmyard for duty as a barn for its congregation must now be virtually a minus quantity.

Near where I sat, behind that gaunt ash at the roadside, stood the one eccentric feature of the scene. At first glance, I thought I was drawing a thatched bus stop but no bus ever runs to or from Ridley. Inspection revealed a newly restored, closed well-head, protected from the weather by crisp, fresh thatch and bearing the inscription 'Bowdler's Well, 1810'.* Can it be that the Friends extend their benefactions beyond the churchyard wall? Who else could it be in lonely Ridley?

* A subsequent visit to nearby Ash, which has long shared the same vicar as Ridley, revealed a 19th century Bowdler on the register of incumbents. A latter day Moses, maybe, striking water with his divining rod?

STANSTED
St. Mary

At the stony place

Stansted church, as presently constituted, dates from 1312 but was restored in 1883 and this is fairly obvious from the pristine condition of the flintwork. It still looks like the work of yesterday and the effects of 100 years of weather have yet to stamp their mellowing magic on the fabric. There has been an earlier building and the evidence for this is claimed to be two smallish, grass covered, piles of flint near the ancient yew. It strains one's incredulity to accept that unneeded stone from the 14th century rebuilding should still remain lying about where the masons left it 600 years ago. These two heaps must surely qualify as one of the most historic rubbish tips in the county and one would not dare to tidy them away now although one would welcome the chance to search for the odd groat or two.

It is a nice little church, comfortably tucked away in a fold in the Downs in the centre of its straggling hamlet. There is nothing particularly remarkable about it but it does retain in place its rood screen and a noticeable acreage of good ledger stones. Two curiosities struck me. The first, the list of vicars begins in 1846. It is my impression that the clergy are always careful to ensure that their names are permanently displayed in their churches. Allowing ten years to the average incumbency, some fifty odd priests have been deprived of recognition; I should be very annoyed if I was one of them. The second oddity to catch my eye, a pair of memorial tablets; one commemorates a 'Woddin', deceased 1632, the other a 'Woddene', deceased 1638. One wouldn't expect such a change in spelling within six short years.

When this version of the church was built, the unhappy Edward II was on the throne and the Hundred Years War with France was only twenty six years away. It makes one pause when driving home in one's car to reflect on the extraordinary contrast between life in the 14th and 20th centuries and yet the church itself remains much as it always has been. I am not certain what moral could be drawn from that thought but I dare say there is one.

However, what attracts one's attention here is not so much the old church. Below the churchyard, where three country lanes meet to create the hub of Stansted, stands a bronze figure of a young man, perhaps an angel, holding aloft in his widespread arms a symbolic frond of palm. It is one of the most striking, distinguished and original war memorials that I have seen. They told me at the pub that in fact the statue had once been stolen and subsequently found abandoned on the North Kent Marshes. How lucky for Stansted to recover its treasure.

EAST FARLEIGH
St. Mary

Fern clearing may be one derivation; the place was called Ferlega in the Domesday Book, 'fer' being the Saxon word for a passage. The passage referred to must be the crossing of the Medway at this point, there being a bridge here in 900 AD. The Saxon bridge has been replaced by the now famous 14th century stone bridge which was the scene of a bitter engagement between the Parliamentary troops under Fairfax and the Royalists as the former made their advance on Maidstone. It is said that the Royalists lost some 1500 killed or taken prisoner; I imagine the Roundhead casualties were correspondingly stiff. Today everyone can swim. At the time of the Civil War, I doubt if many could and that limitation would make a crossing of the river elsewhere impracticable and a frontal assault on the narrow bridge unavoidable. Rather them than me.

The church is high above the bridge on the south bank. Like the first bridge, there has been a church here from before the Conquest. The existing building includes a Saxo-Norman west tower, a 13th century nave, chancel and south chapel to which basic framework was added north and south aisles by a local benefactor in Victoria's reign. One can see the difference in stonework quite clearly; uneven rubble stone in the tower, regular courses of squared eight inch blocks of ragstone, crudely bolstered in the medieval fabric, smoothly trimmed in the Victorian additions. The whole effect, from any angle, is harmonious and one could wish that Einstein's curvature of space would allow one to sketch from two directions at the same time so as to include both west tower and east facade on one flat piece of paper. My chosen view gave me a bonus; from where I sat, behind my chair the sunken road ran past the churchyard wall down to the river and bridge and above, on the far side, I could just make out a gable of the old rectory in which my great, great, great grandfather lived when he was rector of Barming from 1780-1820. A bit more curvature of space and I might have got that in too.

This visit to East Farleigh, as with a previous occasion, was most agreeable. Making a final inspection of the churchyard, I found I was myself under scrutiny by the caretaker (the church had lost some lead from the roof not too long ago). Finding no criminal intent, he opened up and gave me a conducted tour of the interior and we missed nothing of interest. He didn't recognise me but I remembered him for this second visit to his church was virtually a repeat of my first. East Farleigh can confidently expect to escape the worst of today's vandalism, as it deserves to, with such an admirable, aimiable and vigilant guardian.

St. Peter and St. Paul

Teston church is a rare example of the classical period amongst Kent's village churches. It is cruciform in plan having been built, more probably rebuilt, in 1736 by its then patron who lived in the adjacent Barham Court. (What can have been the objection to its predecessor, one wonders; decay possibly?) The classical impression is conveyed by the Georgian style doorways at each cardinal face and one feels that the designer owed something to Christopher Wren or Inigo Jones. I have been here twice, never gained admittance and not yet seen a soul in the churchyard so my knowledge of the interior is confined to Pevsner; he doesn't make much of it and I am surprised by no mention of any memorial to Sir Philip Boteler, the patron. I suppose the church could be said to be his memorial.

The church is very happily positioned two fields or so above the north bank of the Medway. It faces a neat, sequestered green, is bordered by a period farm on one side, by period cottages on the other and is backed by the park and entrance lodge to Barham Court. No harm can come to Teston church. In choosing my composition, I could not resist a glimpse of the chancel end with that tablet, cartouche more properly, below the east window. To be exact, it is the inscription which I found irresistible and is here reproduced:—

While Firm Integrity
Unaffected zeal for Public good
Steady contempt of Self Interest
Tender attention to each social duty
Benevolence to the whole Human Race
And humble Piety to God
Are held in estimation:
The Memory of the Rev. James Ramsay
(Whose earthly Reliques are here deposited)
Will Claim respect
Mingled with sorrow that his labours
Were no longer spared
To the Poor, the Friendless and the Oppressed
For each of whom
Of whatever Clime or Colour
His Christian love and generous exertions
Not (sic) disappointment could exhaust
Calumny slacken
Or Perfection Abate
(He died the 20th July, 1789, AET 56)

Such an eulogistic epitaph may smack of extravagant hyperbole but, in the case of the Rev. Ramsay, who with Wilberforce was instrumental in founding the movement for the abolition of slavery, it is very likely no more than the truth.

Mereworth, three miles up the Maidstone road from Hadlow, has a most distin-guished and interesting but uncharacteristic Kentish church. In the 1740s when John Fane, 7th Earl of Westmorland decided to build his palladian mansion, Mere-worth Castle, he found the medieval church an obstacle to his plans. So down came the church (what was the Bishop of Rochester thinking of?) and instead, by way of reparation, the earl paid for the construction of a less obtrusive, replacement church, more in the centre of the village. And a very handsome reparation it was too; he did the village proud and no-one could regret the passing of the original.

The new church is a simple rectangle with sixteen massive Doric columns sup-porting the barrel roof and twenty matching half columns embedded in the sur-rounding walls. With no separate chancel, the unusual impression created is that of a Grecian temple elaborately equipped and decorated. Inserted within the west end of the temple is the distinctive tower, thus making on one side, a private chapel, on the other the vestry. Securely barred against unauthorised entry, the chapel houses the brasses, a recumbent knight and the exuberant tomb of an earlier Fane, all of which were brought from the old church and installed here. Opposite in the vestry are various memorials to vanished gentlefolk and one to the first holder of the V.C., awarded in 1854 and, more curiously, a ledger stone to someone from 'Northton-shire' (Northamptonshire?) who died in 1654.

Despite the idiosyncratic interior, it is the tower which holds the attention at Mereworth. My sketch shows the top half only — problems of perspective again. Hidden by the yews is a semi-circular pillared portico giving access to the circular base of the tower through which one enters the church. Here one is greeted by an elegant pair of circular staircases, one ascending to the musicians' gallery, the other to the bellringers' chamber above. The tower continues upwards with a square section for the clock, followed by an octagonal section for the belfry below a lantern supporting the tall needle spire. I think that is roughly the right sequence. It is a moulded, corniced and decorated construction in darkened sandstone, said to be modelled on one of the city churches; it can be seen for miles around and has long defied my sketching pen.

The churchyard is more open than most and well stocked with tombstones. Several old headstones attracted my attention, one being dated 1750, others older but indecypherable and presumably pre-dating this church. I can only suppose that, along with the interior memorials of the old church, the graveyard furniture was transferred also. One hopes that it was only the headstones which were moved and that the departed were allowed to remain undisturbed in their graves — to become in the 1980s the unknown and possibly unsuspected tenants of an Arab sheik.

Yalding church, with its distinctive onion dome cap on its stair turret, is a frustrating subject to draw. From whatever direction one looks, there is some obstacle to interrupt the composition. I now know this church and village fairly well but I have not yet found a satisfactory solution to the problem. On the occasion of my sketch in this book I was driven in desperation to the flood plain of the River Beult immediately upstream of the medieval Town Bridge. The track to my vantage point bluntly discouraged 'trespassers' and from it my composition makes too much of the foreground willows at the expense of the church but at least I managed to include the onion. However it was not long before a smallish girl approached and made it clear that I should move on as I was worrying the distant grazing horses and barking dogs. In view of the 'trespassers' notice I did not think I could argue and so took myself off — fortunately with enough of a sketch to serve as my rough. Yalding church deserves a more thorough treatment than I was allowed to give it.

It is a very fine church in a village that unites three of the five Kent rivers for which it provides two medieval stone bridges. The church is set in a substantial churchyard, liberally endowed with ancient yews (plus one ginkgo) and ageing headstones. I would have liked to draw the latter but dappled ranks of weathered 18th and 19th century headstones do not constitute a portrait of a church. The church itself is built of ragstone, irregularly in the unbuttressed 13th century tower, and of coursed dressed stones elsewhere. There are two porches, one now well out of the vertical, and two transepts; most windows are Perpendicular but there are earlier existing and blocked lancets in the chancel. The illustrated 'Walkround Guide' compiled by the children of Class One at the Yalding C of E primary school claims that parts of the church, particularly the lower part of the tower, pre-date the Conquest. I don't doubt that they are right.

Inside the church is spacious, chiefly given over to the memorials of two families, one of which contributed four vicars in succession to cover a span of precisely 100 years from 1759 to 1859. Amongst other things, the church is noteworthy for an unobtrusive glass engraving by Lawrence Whistler on one of the chancel lancets to commemorate Edmund Blunden, Yalding's native poet. Equally 20th century but more conspicuous is a centre section of the barrel roof, ornamented by a pattern of carved bosses and painted bright red — by the present vicar's sons it is said. Very high up and not something I would ever have liked to attempt. I hope their effort receives its proper reward in heaven; it certainly embellishes their father's church in the present day.

HUNTON
St. Mary

Hunta's farmstead

Hunton church can hardly be said to be the focus of a country village. There is a scattering of modern cottages along the road that borders the churchyard, some farm houses here and there and a few nearby mansions, in one of which a Liberal prime minister once lived. So Hunton, although a backwater today, has had its big fish in the past.

The church is basically 13th century in origin with Victorian additions. The nave walls on the north side give a very distinct impression of crumbling antiquity as does the base of the tower and the tombstones clustered around. One of the table tombs in the foreground of my drawing bore the legible date of 1654 which, I believe is extremely early for churchyard memorials. Also visible are examples of those enigmatic, dateless, little tombstones in the shape of a head and shoulders. Their inscriptions are so eroded by time as to be indecipherable but nonetheless they exert an intriguing air of mysterious anonymity which always makes them a challenge to draw. Hunton church is well stocked with those and other headstones which suggests to me that there were once many more people living round about than there are today. It is altogether too elaborate a church for a few farms, a few commuters and a few council cottages, pace those who presently form the parish.

The interior of Hunton church, by no means uninteresting or undecorated, is dominated by an outsize hanging monument towering above the pulpit. When the Friends of Kent Churches held their 1984 AGM in Hunton church much learned discussion was devoted to the possible identity of the artist who created the extravaganza. I doubt, however, whether the Thomas Fane of 1692, whom it commemorates, would be so charmed by the attention paid to the sculptor and the total lack of interest in himself. It is a paradox that memorials put up in memory of some worthy have now commonly come to enjoy more attention than is given to their subjects.

As far as I am aware (not far) Catholic churches on the Continent mostly employed artists to glorify the Holy Family and the saints, not the secular departed. Here, in Kent at any rate, we follow the opposite practice and ignore sacred subjects in favour of the mundane. At the risk of sounding sacrilegious and offending the heavenly hosts, I must confess that I prefer the English custom.

JAS

A dear little church in a minuscule village on the road to nowhere not far from Hadlow. Sharing the boundary of the village cricket ground with the pub and the orchards and farm buildings of a typical fruit farm, the church fields at extra-cover or square leg depending on which end is bowling.

Originally Saxon, it has at the foot of a dumpy tower those minimal double-splayed windows, which are the architectural signature of the Saxons. The nave and north chapel are 13th-14th century and of size appropriate to the parish roll then and today. But I suppose interest in the church must be primarily historical and concentrate on the chapel which was founded as a chantry by Sir John Colepepper in 1408 under a licence from Henry IV; presumably granted in one of that monarch's spare moments from quelling his turbulent barons. Sir John, at this time, gave his manor here to the Knights Hospitallers of St. John of Jerusalem — out of piety and gratitude, or more probably, penitence? — and the Knights' 'Commandery', a substantial timber framed house now known as Dukes Place, still stands at the entrance to the village.

In due course, Sir John and his lady were interred in their chantry but, with the dissolution of the monastries by Henry VIII, the chantry perforce lost its medieval role and instead became the private pew of the owners of Oxenhoath, West Peckham's great house. Conversion of the chantry into a family pew called for the construction of enclosed seating above the Colepepper vault; something the founder did not bargain for and would not have permitted, I feel sure. Nevertheless all went well with this storied arrangement until restoration was undertaken in 1890. It was then proposed that access to the private pew should be by external door rather than across the chancel as had been the practice for over 200 years. The Gearys to whom the raised pew then belonged resisted this encroachment of their established privilege and a lawsuit was brought by the church authorities to deprive them of their right of way. I am happy to say that the defendants won the case but less happy to record that there are no longer Gearys at West Peckham to exercise their lawful prerogative.

My view of the church, perhaps not the best available, was dictated by a slight link with its east end where my great, great, great aunt, Christiana Noble, lies buried beneath a massive, horizontal slate slab. Her in-laws keep her company and rest below the row of headstones shown immediately under the chancel window. Now, over 100 years later, it gives me a family feeling of satisfaction to include their memorials in my rendering of their parish church.

DODDINGTON   *Dudda's farmstead*
The Beheading of St. John the Baptist

Doddington church is exactly the sort of withdrawn country church that I like and perhaps Edward I thought the same for he came here in 1305 before he went north to hammer the Scots for the last time. The church is small, a blend of flint and patches of faded cement rendering with the most endearingly ridiculous, weather-boarded tower. The structure of double nave, chancel and chapel dates from 1100 but the wooden tower with its preposterous boarded battlemented parapet is a 19th century replacement of an earlier version which was damaged by lightening in 1650. It is remarkable how often these medieval churches suffered from 'acts of God'; if I was an insurance assessor I might be tempted to accuse the Almighty of criminal negligence.*

Inside, the church has that evocative odour that goes with sanctity and venerable old churches and which brings the past alive so vividly. Here is this tiny, unassuming flint church and yet it has experienced and outlasted the times of the Normans, the Plantagenets, the Tudors, the Stuarts and the Hanoverians; the Wars of the Roses, the Civil War, the struggles for empire, the industrial revolution, the great European wars of the 20th century and the years of retreat from empire; such a cavalcade of the nation's triumphs and tribulations has there been but outwardly the church remains today much as it was 600 years ago when Edward came. We are light years apart in material life styles and beliefs but Edward's generation and ours would nonetheless be united in appreciating this enduring little church. 600 years from now, it could still be delighting the eye.

Architecturally, of course, it is of interest with primitive lancet windows, one particularly celebrated, 14th century wall paintings in the splays of the chancel windows, a double squint, and a group of handsome ledger stones in the south chapel. As always these dark slabs, with their elegant calligraphy and unabashed engraved coats of arms, defy the years more successfully than their opposite numbers outside in the churchyard. At Doddington, the centre stone has mysteriously had its inscription deliberately obliterated. The coat of arms remains undefaced so presumably it was only the individual and not the family who had to be rendered anonymous. I wonder what sin can have given rise to this desecration.

Another oddity of Doddington is its dedication. Charing, about five miles away as the crow flies, claims the stone on which St. John the Baptist was beheaded. Why therefore was Doddington so dedicated? There must be a reason; perhaps the stone, if it exists, was moved to Doddington and that was what drew Edward I, an old crusader himself, to this church in 1305. It is an intriguing thought for really Doddington is altogether too peaceful and demure for so brutal a dedication; St. Francis of Assissi would be more appropriate to its rural innocence.

* Oddly enough, less than a month after I made this critical observation, York Cathedral suffered a similar accident and was severely damaged by fire.

BARMING
St. Margaret

I cannot resist including Barming in my treasury of Kent country churches. It lies surrounded by fields and separate from its village above the Medway, five miles from Hadlow, and now in grave danger of being engulfed by any further westward extension of Maidstone.

The church is a simple combination of nave and chancel with a conspicuous needle-spired west tower. That it is included in most lists of Kent churches owes less to its architectural merits than to some early carved bench ends, said to be German in origin, and dating from about 1300. None of the expert comments explain why these continental carvings are found in this unassuming village church or when they were placed there; these are the questions to ask and to answer, I suggest.

However, it is not its attractive or vulnerable setting above the Medway that prompts the inclusion of Barming church in my record of exploration. The reason is because the rector here from 1780 to 1820, one Mark Noble, was my great, great, great grandfather and I know something about him. His interests would seem to have been more literary than religious and, to judge from his account of his own family, not too attractive in his prejudices. Amongst other works, he wrote a history of Barming; the manuscript is kept in the Maidstone museum and the officials there insist on an appointment before one can see it; such is bureaucracy but one must admit it is well-intentioned. My remembrance of Noble's history of Barming is one of sustained criticism of his more important parishioners, omission of matters religious, and the whole enlivened by endearing little sketches by his deprecated son. There is a minimum of historical interest recorded and, in this respect, Mark Noble resembles his Kent contemporary, Edward Hasted, whose celebrated history of Kent could almost be described as an estate agent's catalogue.

My sketch of Barming hardly does justice to its setting amongst the fields and orchards which descend to the Medway. Opposite on the right bank is the church of East Farleigh and, less than two miles upstream, are the churches of West Farleigh and Teston; all four overlooking this brief stretch of the river. It is still undeniably beautiful and, in the Middle Ages when these churches were built, as well as being a magnet for the clergy, the Medway must have been important as a highway. More than one of my ancestors has been connected with the Church but none flourished so close to my present home as Mark Noble. His proximity provides a peculiarly comforting feeling in my declining years.

Last but not least in my catalogue of Kent country churches, St. Mary's, Hadlow.
This is a much restored and remodelled village church of Saxo-Norman origins
which, in fact, celebrated its millenium in 1975. The Saxon part is the foot of the
tower, the Norman part the rest of the tower, with the remainder of the church
entirely overlaid by unfortunate improvements in the 1850s. Inside the church is
rather bare and barn-like due to the destruction of many of the old monuments
during the 19th century rebuilding. In passing, as a compliment to the 20th century,
I must record my opinion that the recent redecoration of the chancel has vastly
improved that difficult part of this church. One memorial the Victorians overlooked,
or could not efface, is three tiny and inconspicuous scratched crosses on the stone
jambs of the Saxon doorway at the foot of the tower. Two of these chiselled
graffiti are attributed to Nicholas de Hadloe and his son who were at the seige of
Acre with Richard I. I understand the theory to be that the vertical score was made
on departure for the Crusade with the cross being triumphantly completed by the
horizontal arm as a thanksgiving for a safe return. It is a romantic fancy and whether
it is true or not cannot now be settled but it is true enough that these two inch
crosses are there on the Saxon doorway.

It is impossible to achieve a satisfactory overall view of Hadlow church but the
aspect which I have depicted here is the one that I see everyday from my garden
which is separated from the churchyard by no more than a narrow sunken footpath.
My drawing avoids the Victorian additions but includes the pleasant churchyard
which incidentally is currently kept in apple-pie order. What is omitted, as being
largely but not entirely obscured, is the dominant feature of the village and the
countryside around, Hadlow Tower. This is an 170 foot high Gothic folly tower that
stands beyond the church in what remains of the so-called Hadlow Castle. The
mansion has gone but the folly remains, a monument to the eccentricities of a local
squire and the limited openings available to him for the dissipation of accumulated
wealth. In an egalitarian society, such conspicuous expenditure would not enjoy
general approval but, nevertheless, I cannot imagine that there is any inhabitant of
Hadlow today who does not take pride in our outstanding extravagance.

Hadlow church completes this account of my absorbing and fascinating exploration of a few of the many Kent country churches. What to do next is the question.
In this material world it is a conundrum that one should find unworldly architecture
so irrestible but possibly the one is a consequence of the other.